9/29/00

The Best
Short Stories of

D. H. LAWRENCE

Selected and simplified by
Michael Woolf

Longman

Longman Group UK Limited,
Longman House, Burnt Mill, Harlow,
Essex CM20 2JE, England
and Associated Companies throughout the world

First published 1987

ISBN 0-582-52646-9

Set in Century Schoolbook 9/11 Linotron 202
Produced by Longman Group (F.E.) Ltd
Printed in Hong Kong

Contents

Introduction   1

The White Stocking   3

The Shadow in the Rose Garden   17

Odour of Chrysanthemums   25

The Prussian Officer   37

The Horse Dealer's Daughter   49

The Blind Man   63

Mother and Daughter   73

Glossary   87

Questions   88

Introduction

David Herbert Lawrence is one of a small group of writers
who helped change literature in this century. He did not
experiment very much with the language or the manner in
which stories are told but he was revolutionary in the way
in which he wrote about the complicated nature of the
feelings between people. In these stories, the idea of a
mysterious power deep within the self is seen, over and over
again, controlling the way people act towards each other.
This is shown in the sexual relationships between men and
women in stories like *The Horse Dealer's Daughter*, *Mother
and Daughter* or *The White Stocking*. However, the feelings
between men are also controlled by the same sort of
mysterious force in *The Blind Man* or *The Prussian Officer*.

Love, in all its many forms, is an important subject for
Lawrence. It is a kind of struggle for power between the
women in *Mother and Daughter* and, as in that story, he
frequently shows love as coming very close to hate. This is
particularly true when he describes the terrible power of
jealousy in *The Shadow in the Rose Garden* and *The White
Stocking*. The closeness of hate to love is also shown in the
horror of the story *The Prussian Officer*. Lawrence's view of
human feelings is a deeply complicated and rich one.

Another important subject for Lawrence is class. He was
born in 1885, the son of a miner in Eastwood, a village in
Nottinghamshire. His mother was a middle-class woman
and, therefore, in his own family Lawrence recognised the
deep differences between the classes. That is, of course, a
very English concern which is found throughout our
literature. In his novel *Sons and Lovers*, he wrote about his
own childhood and, in these stories, the same interest in
class is very clear. The fact that the doctor in *The Horse
Dealer's Daughter* is from a different class is important, as it
is in *The Shadow in the Rose Garden*. The problem of class
comes between the lovers in both of those stories. His

interest in the subject is also shown in *Odour of Chrysan-themums* where he describes the poverty and suffering of the miners and their families.

His knowledge of the conditions of industrial England is also shown in these stories, as it was in his famous novel *Lady Chatterly's Lover*. He saw industry as bringing dark-ness and dirt to the natural world. Nature is destroyed by the smoke of factories. Industry also separates people from their real, instinctive feelings. Lawrence believed deeply in the importance of human instinct, and he believed that industry brought a darkness that destroyed both nature and the connection between people and their own true instincts.

Lawrence is most famous for his novels but he also wrote poetry, criticism and, of course, short stories. He was also an artist. His work was often disliked by the law because of the honest and open way in which he discussed sex. He was not allowed to show his paintings, and *Lady Chatterly's Lover* was not sold in England until 1960. The fact that we can now read Lawrence so easily, and that his work can be bought more or less everywhere, is a sign of how much the world has changed. We should not forget how much we owe to Lawrence for helping to make that change happen.

In his later years, Lawrence escaped from what he saw as the darkness of industrial England. He travelled widely particularly in Italy and Mexico. In those countries, he wrote about the distant past, about the world before it had been spoilt by factories and machines. That writing reminds us, as these stories do, of the deep, instinctive nature of man just below the surface of what we call civilisation. He died abroad in 1930 at the age of fourty-four.

These stories are an introduction to his work. They have been changed a little to make them easier to read, but the style and energy of Lawrence's writing remains. I hope that they will be just the beginning in your enjoyment of one of the most important writers of this century.

Michael Woolf

The White Stocking

This story was written in 1907 and is about jealousy, violence, pain and love. It also shows, though, how the sexual instinct is near to the surface in ordinary social events. The dance between Sam Adams and Elsie Whiston is described in a way that makes it sound very much like love-making. The reader is also shown how close love and hatred really are as Ted moves between violence and pity. As often in these stories, Lawrence raises the question of power in the relationship between men and women. Who holds who in their grasp?

"I'M GETTING UP, TEDDY," said Elsie Whiston, and she sprang out of bed quickly.

"What's the matter?" asked her husband, Ted Whiston.

"Nothing. Can't I get up?" she replied lightly.

It was about seven o'clock, scarcely light yet in the cold bedroom. Ted lay still and looked at his wife. She was a pretty little thing, with her thick, short black hair unbrushed and untidy. He watched her as she dressed quickly, throwing her clothes about her. He watched the quickness and softness of her young shoulders, calmly, like a husband, and lovingly.

They had been married two years. But still when she had gone out of the room, he felt as if all his light and warmth were taken away, he suddenly felt the raw, cold morning. So he rose himself, wondering why she had got up so early. Usually, she lay in bed as late as she could.

Ted dressed himself and went downstairs. He was a shapely young fellow of about twenty-eight, sleepy now and easy with well-being. He heard the water running, and she began to whistle. He loved the quick way she washed the

3

cups for breakfast.

"Teddy," she cried.

"What?"

"Light a fire, quick."

She wore an old jacket of black silk pinned across her breast. But one of the sleeves, a little torn, showed some delightful pink upper-arm.

"Why don't you sew your sleeve up?" he said, suffering from the sight of the bare soft flesh.

"Where?" she cried, looking around. "Nuisance," she said, seeing the gap, then with light fingers went on drying the cups.

Suddenly a noise was heard at the door down the passage.

"I'll go," cried Elsie, and she was gone down the hall.

The postman was a red-faced man who had been a soldier. He smiled widely, handing her some small parcels.

"They've not forgotten you," he said.

"No – lucky for them," she said, with a shake of her head. But she was interested only in her mail this morning. It was St Valentine's Day. Slowly, as if she didn't know anyone was there, she closed the door in his face, continuing to look at the addresses on her letters.

She tore open the thin envelope. There was a Valentine card. She smiled and dropped it on the floor. In a small white box, there was a silk handkerchief. She gently put it aside. The third envelope contained a long white stocking. She shook it out. In the little cold toe of the stocking, there was a small box. She looked inside and, with a little flash of pleasure, lifted a pair of pearl earrings from the small box, and went to the mirror. She put them on, looking at herself sideways in the glass.

Then the pearl earrings hung under her rosy, small ears. She shook her head sharply to see them swing. Then she stood still to look at herself. Catching her own eye, she could not help laughing at herself.

Ted had made the fire burn, so he came to look for her. When she heard him, she started round quickly, guiltily.

She was watching him with thoughtful blue eyes when he appeared.

He did not see much, in his sleepy morning warmth. He gave her, as ever, a feeling of warmth and slowness. His eyes were very blue, very kind, his manner simple.

"What have you got?" he asked.

"Valentines," she said, turning to show him the silk handkerchief.

"Who's that from?" he replied.

"It's a Valentine," she cried. "How do I know who it's from?"

"I'll bet you know," he said.

"Ted! — I don't!" she cried, beginning to shake her head, then stopping because of the earrings.

He stood still a moment, displeased.

"They've no right to send you Valentines, now," he said.

"Ted? — Why not? You're not jealous, are you?"

He looked around and saw the white stocking lying on a chair.

"Is this another?" he said.

"No, that's a sample," she said. "There's only a card."

He looked at it solemnly.

"Fools!" he said, and went out of the room.

She flew upstairs and took off the earrings. When she returned, he was kneeling before the fire, blowing on the coals. The skin of his face was red, but his neck was white and smooth. She hung her arms round his neck as he knelt there. He smiled at her.

Over breakfast she grew serious. He did not notice.

"Teddy!" she said at last.

"What?" he asked.

"I told you a lie," she said.

His soul stirred uneasily.

"Oh yes," he said calmly.

She was not satisfied. He ought to be more moved.

"Yes," she said.

He cut a piece of bread.

"Was it a good one?" he asked.

5

She was angry. Then she considered – *was* it a good one? Then she laughed.

"No," she said, "it wasn't very good."

"Ah!" he said easily, but with a steady strength of fondness for her in his voice. "Get it out then."

It became a little more difficult.

"You know that white stocking," she said seriously, "I told you a lie. It wasn't a sample. It was a Valentine."

"Then why did you say it was a sample?" he said. But he knew this weakness of hers. The touch of anger in his voice frightened her.

"I was afraid you'd be angry," she said weakly.

There was a pause. He was considering one or two things in his mind.

"And who sent it?" he asked.

"I can guess," she said, "though there wasn't a word with it . . ."

"And *who* do you guess it is," he asked, with a ringing of anger in his voice.

"I suspect it's Sam Adams," she said, with a little annoyed innocence.

Ted was silent for a moment.

"Fool!" he said. "And why did he send just one stocking?"

"I suppose he thinks it'll make a pair with the one he sent last year."

"Why, did he send one then?"

"Yes. I thought you'd be wild if you knew."

His jaw set rather angrily.

Presently he rose, and went to wash himself, rolling back his sleeves and pulling open his shirt at the breast. As she hurried about, clearing the table, she loved the way in which he stood washing himself. He was such a man. She liked to see his neck shining with water. It amused her and pleased her and excited her. He was so sure, so permanent, he had her so completely in his power. It gave her a delightful sense of freedom. Within his grasp, she could move about excitingly.

He turned around to her, his face red from the cold water,

his eyes fresh and very blue.

"You haven't been seeing anything of him, have you?" he asked roughly.

"Yes," she answered, after a moment, as if caught guilty. "He got into the bus with me, and he invited me for a drink at the Royal Hotel."

"And did you?" he asked.

"Yes," she replied, feeling like a criminal before the court.

The blood came up into his neck and face, he stood motionless, dangerous.

"It was cold, and it was such fun to go into the Royal," she said.

He turned away from her to put on his tie. He was ready to go and he came to kiss her. He would be miserable all day if he went without. She allowed herself to be kissed. Her face was wet under his lips, and his heart burned. She hurt him so deeply. And she felt anger, and did not quite forgive him.

In a moment she went upstairs to her earrings. They looked so sweet! She wore them all morning in the house. And she was happy, and very pretty. She was excited all day. She did not think about her husband. In her imagination she wandered far and wide, but at night she would always come home to him.

Meanwhile Ted went about his work, but all the time his heart was anxious for her, uncertain and uneasy.

II

She had worked for Sam Adams before she was married. He was a well-dressed, heavy man with a large brown moustache and a great fondness for girls. And Elsie, quick and pretty, had a great attraction for him. But she was in love with Ted and they planned to get married.

Every Christmas Sam Adams gave a party for his workers, and two years ago Elsie and Ted had gone to the party for the last time.

7

She had been very proud of herself in her blue silk dress. Ted had called for her. They were rather late and she waited a moment in the door of the brightly lighted room. Many people were moving within the shining lights, the full skirts of the women floating, the white ties of the men bowing above. Then she entered the light.

In an instant Sam Adams was coming forward, lifting both his arms in welcome. There was a continuous red laugh on his face.

"So you've come late, have you," he shouted, "like royalty?"

He seized her hands and led her forward. He opened his mouth wide when he spoke, and the effect of the warm, dark opening beneath the brown moustache was disturbing.

Ted did not dance and Sam took his chance to dance with Elsie for most of the evening. He was an excellent dancer. He seemed to draw her close into him by some male warmth of attraction, so that she became all soft to him, flowing to his form. She was just carried in a kind of strong, warm flood, her feet moved of themselves, and only the music threw her away from him, threw her back to him, to his grasp, in his strong form moving against her, stirring her blood.

When it was over, he was pleased and his eyes shone in a way that excited her and yet had nothing to do with her. Yet his eyes held her. He did not speak to her. He only looked straight into her eyes in a curious way that disturbed her delightfully and fearfully. It left her partly cold. She was not carried away.

She went to find Ted who was playing cards.

"I do wish you could dance," she said.

"Well, I can't," he said. "So enjoy yourself."

She put her hand on his shoulder, looking at his cards.

"But I would enjoy it better if I could dance with you."

He didn't answer but threw down two cards. It moved him more strongly than was comfortable, to have her hand on his shoulder, her curls touching his ears, while she was excited by another man. It made the blood flame over him.

At that moment Sam Adams appeared, rosy and cheerful, as if half drunk with the music. In his eye the curious light shone. He laughed, bowed, and offered her his arm.

She went almost helplessly, carried along with him, unwilling yet delighted. After the first few steps, she felt herself slipping away from herself. She lay in the arm of the steady, close man with whom she was dancing and she seemed to swim away out of touch with the room, into him. His fingers seemed to search into her flesh. Every moment, and every moment, she felt she would give way completely. But he carried her around the room in the dance, and his warmth seemed to come closer into her, nearer, till it would pass right through her, and she would be a liquid to him.

It was wonderful. When it was over, she was only half awake, and was scarcely breathing. She stood with him in the middle of the room as if she were alone. He bent over her. She expected his lips on her bare shoulder, and waited. Yet they were not alone, they were not alone. It was cruel.

"It was good, wasn't it, my darling?" he said to her, low and delighted. His voice attracted her irresistibly. Yet why was she conscious of some part shut off in her? She pressed his arm, and he led her towards the dining room.

In the dining room Ted was carrying coffee for some of the older ladies. When he came over to her, she saw his strong, young man's figure before her.

"Have you finished your cards?" she asked.

"Yes," he replied. "Aren't you getting tired of dancing?"

"Not a bit," she said.

He sat beside her. There was something shapely about him as he sat, about his knees, and his clear figure. She put her hand on his knee.

"It's nearly one o'clock," he said.

"Is it?" she answered. It meant nothing to her.

"Should we be going?" he said. She was silent. For the first time for an hour or more a little of her usual consciousness returned. She resisted it.

"What for?" she said.

"I thought you might have had enough," he said.

9

"Why?" she said.

"We've been here since nine."

That was no answer, no reason. It meant nothing to her. She sat apart from him. Across the room Sam Adams glanced at her. She sat there open to him.

"You don't want to be too free with Sam Adams," Ted said, cautiously, suffering. "You know what he is."

"What do you mean — free?" she asked.

"Why — you don't want to have too much to do with him."

She sat silent. He was forcing her into consciousness of her position. But he could not get hold of her feelings, to change them. She had a curious desire that he should not.

"I like him," she said.

"What do you find to like in him?" he said with a hot heart.

"I don't know — but I like him," she said.

She had promised to dance again with Sam Adams. As she went forward with him to take her place, she pulled out her handkerchief. The music sounded. Everybody was ready. Sam Adams stood with his body near her, attracting her to him. She shook out her handkerchief and it fell from her hand. With pain, she saw that she had taken a white stocking instead of a handkerchief. For a second it lay on the floor, a twist of white stocking. Then, in an instant, Adams picked it up, with a little, surprised laugh of victory.

"That'll do for me," he whispered — seeming to take possession of her. And he quickly put the stocking in his trouser pocket, and offered her his handkerchief.

The dance began. She felt weak and faint, as if her will were turned to water. A heavy sense of loss came over her. She could not help herself anymore. But it was peace.

When the dance was over, Ted came to her.

"What was it you dropped?" he asked.

"I thought it was my handkerchief — I'd taken a stocking by mistake," she said.

"And he's got it?"

"Yes."

"What does he mean by that?"

She lifted her shoulders.

"Are you going to let him keep it?"

There was a long pause.

"Shall I get it from him?" he asked, his face flaming, and his blue eyes going hard with opposition.

"No," she said, pale. "I don't want you to say anything about it."

"You'll let him keep it, then?"

She sat silent and made no form of answer.

"What do you mean by it?" he said, dark with fury. And he started up.

"No!" she cried. "Ted!" And she caught hold of him.

It made him black with anger.

"Why?" he said.

Then something about her mouth was pitiful to him. He didn't understand, but he felt that she must have her reasons.

"Then I'm not stopping here," he said. "Are you coming with me?"

She rose silently, and they went out of the room. In a few moments they were in the street.

"What the hell do you mean?" he said in a black fury.

She went at his side, in silence.

"That great pig!" he added.

Then they went a long time in silence through the frozen, deserted darkness of the town. She felt that she could not go indoors. They were getting near her house.

"I don't want to go home," she suddenly cried. "I don't want to go home."

He looked at her.

"Why don't you?" he said.

"I don't want to go home," was all that she could cry.

"Well, we can walk a bit further," he said.

She was silent again. They passed out of the town into the fields. He held her by the arm – they couldn't speak.

"What's the matter?" he asked at length, puzzled.

She began to cry again.

At last he took her in his arms, to comfort her. He kissed

her wet face and held her. He was puzzled and tender and miserable.

At length she became quiet. Then he kissed her, and she put her arms round him, and held him very tight, as if in fear and pain. He held her in his arms wondering.

"Ted!" she whispered. "Ted!"

"What, my love?" he answered, becoming also afraid.

"Be good to me," she cried. "Don't be cruel to me."

"No, my pet," he said, suffering. "Why?"

"Oh, be good to me," she cried bitterly.

And he held her very safe, and his heart was white-hot with love for her. His mind was astonished. He could only hold her against his chest that was white-hot with love and belief in her. So she was his again.

III

She left her job at Adams's and, a few weeks later, she and Ted were married. She loved him fiercely and he felt sure of her. He had found himself in this love.

They spoke once or twice about the white stocking but he was impatient and angry, and could not bear to consider the matter. So it was left.

She was quite happy at first, carried away by her love for her husband. Then gradually she got used to him. He was always the ground of her happiness, but she got used to him, as to the air she breathed. He never got used to her in the same way.

Inside of marriage she found her freedom. She had no responsibility for herself. Her husband must look after that. She was free to get what she could out of her time.

So that, when she met Sam Adams after some months, she was not unkind to him. She knew he was in love with her. And she could not help playing with that, though she cared nothing for the man.

When Valentine's day came, almost a year after her wedding, a white stocking arrived with a little brooch. She said nothing about it. She kept it.

Now she had the pearl earrings. They were a more valuable present. She would say she got them from her mother. And she was extraordinarily pleased. As for Sam Adams, even if he saw her wearing them, he would keep their secret. What fun if he saw her wearing his earrings!

Ted came home tired and unhappy. All day the male nature in him had been uneasy. She was curiously against him. Sometimes now she mocked him, and cut him off. He didn't understand this and it angered him deeply. She was uneasy before him.

"What did you do with that white stocking?" he asked out of a dark silence. His voice was strong.

"I put it in a drawer," she replied lightly.

"Why didn't you put it on the fire?" he said.

He became silent. She, unable to move him, ran away upstairs, leaving him smoking by the fire. Again she tried on the earrings. Then another idea came to her. She drew on the white stockings, both of them.

Presently she came down in them. Her husband still sat immovable, staring into the fire.

"Look!" she said. "They'll do beautifully."

And she picked up her skirts to her knees, and twisted round, looking at her pretty legs in the neat stockings.

"Don't they look nice?" she said. "One from last year and one from this. Save you buying a pair."

He filled with unreasonable fury, and took the pipe from his mouth.

"Put your skirts down and don't make a fool of yourself," he said.

"Why a fool of myself?" she asked.

And she began to dance slowly round the room, kicking up her feet, half-mocking, in a dancer's fashion. Almost fearfully, yet determined, she kicked up her legs at him, singing as she did so.

"You little fool," he said. "You'll burn those stockings, I'm telling you." He was angry. His face became dark, he kept his head bent. She stopped dancing.

"I won't," she said. "They'll be very useful."

He lifted his head and watched her with dangerous, lighted eyes.

"You'll put them in the fire, I tell you," he said.

It was a war now. She bent forward and put her tongue between her teeth.

"I won't," she sang, "I won't, I won't, I won't."

And she danced around the room doing a high kick to the tune of her words.

"You'd like Sam Adams to know you were wearing them, wouldn't you?"

"Yes, I'd like him to see how nicely they fit me, he might give me some more then."

He knew somehow that she *would* like Sam Adams to see how pretty her legs looked in the white stockings. It made his anger go deep, almost to hatred.

"Have you been having anything to do with him?" he asked.

"I've just spoken to him when I've seen him," she said. "He's not as bad as you would make out."

All his uncontrollable anger was rising. Every one of her sentences stirred him up like a red-hot iron. Soon it would be too much. And she was afraid herself; but she was neither defeated nor controlled.

There was a silence.

"*You're* not going to tell me everything I can and can't do," she said at last.

He lifted his head.

"I tell you this," he said in a low, dangerous voice. "If you have anything to do with Sam Adams, I'll break your neck."

She laughed, high and false.

"You don't know everything," she said with a strange, mocking laugh, "he sent me a brooch and a pair of pearl earrings."

"He what?" said Ted in a suddenly cold voice. His eyes were fixed on her.

"Sent me a pair of pearl earrings and a brooch," she repeated, mechanically, pale to the lips.

And her big, black, childish eyes watched him.

14

He rose slowly and came to her. She watched in terror. Her throat made a small sound, as she tried to scream.

Then, quick as lightning, the back of his hand struck her with a crash across the mouth, and she was thrown back blinded against the wall. The shock shook a strange sound out of her. And then she saw him still coming on, his eyes holding her.

Mad with terror, she raised her hands to cover her eyes, opening her mouth in a silent scream. There was no sound. But the sight of her slowly stopped him. She stood against the wall with open, bleeding mouth, and wide-staring eyes. And his desire to see her bleed, to break her and destroy her, rose from out of his memory. He wanted satisfaction.

But he had seen her standing there, a pitiable, horrified thing, and he turned his face away in shame and sickness. He went and sat heavily in his chair, and a curious ease, almost like sleep, came over his brain.

She walked away from the wall towards the fire, white to the lips, mechanically wiping her small, bleeding mouth. Then, gradually, she began to shake, and she was crying deeply, in grief for herself. Without looking, he saw. It made his mad desire to destroy her come back.

At length he lifted his head. His eyes were fixed on her.

"And why did he give you them?" he asked in a steady voice.

"They came as Valentines," she replied, beaten but not defeated. "The pearl earrings today and the brooch last year."

She felt that now nothing would prevent him if he rose to kill her. She couldn't prevent him any more. They both trembled in the balance, unconscious.

"What have you had to do with him?" he asked in a dead voice.

"I've not had anything to do with him," her voice shook.

"You just kept them because they were jewellery?" he said.

She began to cry again, but he took no notice. She kept wiping her mouth on her handkerchief. He could see the

15

blood. It made him only more sick and tired of the responsibility of it, the violence, the shame.

"Where are the things?" he said.

"They're upstairs," she said. She knew the anger had gone down in him.

"Bring them down," he said.

"I won't," she wept with fury. "You're not going to hit me like that on the mouth."

And she wept again. He looked at her with pity and anger.

"Where are they?" he said.

"They're in the little drawer," she cried.

He went slowly upstairs, found the jewellery, and tied the things up into a box which he addressed to Sam Adams.

When he came back down, she was still crying.

"You'd better go to bed," he said.

She took no notice. He sat by the fire. She still cried.

"I'm sleeping down here," he said. "You can go to bed."

In a few moments she lifted her tear-stained, swollen face and looked at him with eyes all despairing and pitiful. A great flash of pain went over his body. He went over slowly, and very gently took her in his hands. She let herself be taken. Then as she lay against his shoulder, she wept aloud:

"I never meant —"

"My love – my little love – " he cried, his spirit suffering as he held her in his arms.

16

The Shadow in the Rose Garden

This story was written in 1908 and jealousy is again the subject, though it is more complicated here. The young man is from the working class while his wife is from the middle class, and this adds to the gap between them. The woman has also had a previous relationship which deeply troubles the man. The story raises the question of how far we can expect to possess another person. Lawrence's view of war as a terrible waste of life is also shown here

A RATHER SMALL YOUNG MAN sat by the window of a pretty seaside cottage trying to persuade himself that he was reading. It was about half-past eight in the morning. Outside, roses hung in the morning sunshine like little bowls of fire. The young man looked at the table, then at the clock, then at his own big silver watch. Then he rose and looked at the paintings that hung on the walls of the room. He caught sight of his own face in a little mirror, pulled his brown moustache. He was not bad-looking, he felt.

As he went through to the garden, he felt a little uneasy, disturbed. But his jacket was new and he had a well-dressed, self-confident air. He broke off an apple from the old tree in the garden and took a clean, sharp bite. To his surprise, the fruit was sweet. He took another. Then he turned to look at the bedroom windows overlooking the garden. He felt surprised, seeing a woman's figure; but it was only his wife. She was staring across to the sea, not seeing him.

For a moment or two he looked at her, watching her. She

was a good-looking woman, who seemed older than him, rather pale, but healthy, her face dreaming. Her rich brown hair was full on her forehead. She looked apart from him and his world, staring away to the sea. It annoyed her husband that she should be so distant and so unconscious of him. He picked up a small stone and threw it gently at the window. She jumped in surprise, glanced at him with a wild smile, and looked away again. Then almost immediately she left the window. He went indoors to meet her. She had a fine figure, very proud, and wore a soft, white dress.

"I've been waiting long enough," he said.

"For me or for breakfast?" she said lightly. "You know we said nine o'clock. I should have thought you could have slept after the journey."

She moved about examining the room.

"Come," she said, taking his arm, "let's go into the garden till Mrs Coates brings the breakfast tray."

"I hope she'll be quick," he said, pulling his moustache. She gave a short laugh, and leaned on his arm as they went. He had lighted a pipe.

Mrs Coates entered the room as they went down the steps. The old lady watched the newly-married couple walking in an easy, confident manner. They were as tall as each other but, she thought, they were not of the same class. She was above him. He worked in the mines.

The couple came in to breakfast. After the young man had eaten for some time, he rested for a moment and said:

"Are you enjoying it here?"

"I am," she said, "very much. Besides, I am at home here – it's not a strange seaside place to me."

"How long were you here?"

"Two years. But don't say anything about it in the village, Frank. There's nobody I want to meet, particularly, and we should never feel free if they knew me again."

"Why did you come, then?"

"I came to see the place, not the people," she said.

He did not say anything more.

She helped him to another cup of coffee.

18

"Only," she began again, "don't talk about me in the village." She laughed shakily. "I don't want people to remember my past."

"You've had a lot of past, have you?"

"Well," she said, fondly, "you won't give me away, who I am, will you?"

"No," he said, comforting, laughing, "I won't give you away."

He was pleased.

She remained silent. After a moment or two, she lifted her head, saying:

"I've got a lot of little things to do this morning. So you'd better go out by yourself and we'll meet for lunch at one."

He realised that she wanted to be alone so, when she went upstairs, he took his hat and went out on to the cliffs, holding his anger in.

Soon she too came out. She wore a hat with roses and, rather nervously, she put up her sunshade and her face was half-hidden in its coloured shadows. She went along a narrow path that was worn flat by the feet of the fishermen. She seemed to be avoiding her surroundings, hiding in the shadows of her sunshade.

She passed the church and went down the road till she came to a high wall. Under this she went slowly until she came to an open doorway which shone like a picture of light in the dark wall. There in the magic beyond the doorway, patterns of shadow lay on the blue and white path and, beyond that, a green lawn shone. She stepped nervously in, glancing at the house that stood in the shadow. The windows looked black and soulless, the kitchen door stood open. Uncertainly, she took a step forward, and again forward, dreaming, leaning towards the garden beyond.

She had almost reached the corner of the house when a heavy step came through the trees. A gardener appeared before her.

"The garden isn't open today," he said quietly to the attractive woman, who was nervously ready to run.

"Could I just have one little look at the roses?" she asked.

"I don't suppose it would matter," he said, moving aside; "you won't stop long –"

She went forward, forgetting the gardener in a moment. Her face became anxious, her movements eager. Glancing round, she saw that the windows of the house were dark. It looked dead, as if it were used, but not lived in. A shadow seemed to go over her. She went across the lawn towards the garden. Beyond lay the soft blue sea and the black rock between the blue of the sky and the blue of the water. Her face began to shine, caught with joy and pain.

She turned to the garden that shone with sunny flowers. She knew the little corner with the seat beneath the tree. She closed her sunshade and walked slowly among the flowers. All around were roses, growing, hanging, falling.

Slowly she went down one path, wandering, like one who has gone back into the past. Suddenly she was touching some soft red roses, touching them thoughtfully, without knowing, as a mother touches the hand of her child. Then she wandered on. She felt herself in a strange, laughing crowd of roses. It excited her, carried her out of herself. The air was pure scent.

Hastily, she went to a little seat among the white roses, and sat down. She was not herself.

Then she jumped cruelly as a shadow crossed her and a figure moved into her sight. It was a man who had come unheard. The morning was broken, the magic disappeared. He came forward. She stood up. Then, seeing him, the strength went from her and she sank on the seat again.

He was a young man, military in appearance, growing slightly fat. His black hair was smooth and bright. She looked up, whitened to the lips, and saw his eyes. They were black and stared without seeing. They were not a man's eyes. He was coming towards her.

He stared at her and sat down beside her on the seat.

"I don't disturb you – do I?" he said.

She was silent and helpless. She couldn't move. Seeing his hands, with the ring that she knew so well upon the little

20

finger, she felt as if she were going to faint. The whole world was mad. His hands that she had loved so much filled her with horror as they rested now on his strong legs. She sat without moving. She could see his shape, the shape she had loved with all her strength.

"Do you mind if I smoke?" he said. "Perhaps I shall be able to see things more clearly."

She watched his hands with the fine strong fingers. They had always trembled slightly, but now they moved unsteadily and tobacco hung out of the pipe. He talked on, wandering from one thing to another.

She sat and heard him talking. But it was not he. Yet those were the hands she had kissed, there were the shining, strange black eyes she had loved. Yet it was not he. She sat motionless with horror and silence.

"I must go at once," he said. "The birds are coming."

She rose too. He was a good-looking, soldierly fellow, and a madman. Her eyes searched him, and searched him, to see if he would recognise her, if she could discover him.

"You don't know me?" she asked, from the terror of her soul, standing alone.

He looked back at her. She had to bear his eyes. They shone on her with no intelligence. He came closer to her.

"Yes, I do know you," he said, with a mad fixed stare, his face coming closer to hers. Her horror was too great. The powerful madman was coming too near to her.

A man approached, hurrying.

"The garden isn't open this morning," he said.

The madman stopped and looked at him.

"I was just asking this lady to stay to lunch," he said politely. "She is a friend of mine."

The woman turned and walked quickly, blindly, between the sunny roses, out from the garden, past the house with the dead, dark windows, and into the street. As soon as she got back to the cottage she went upstairs, took off her coat, and sat down on the bed. It was as if something had been torn in her so that she couldn't think or feel. She sat completely still.

After a time, she heard the hard tread of her husband below and then his solid footsteps coming near.

He entered, healthy, rather pleased, with an air of confidence about him. She moved stiffly and he hesitated.

"What's the matter?" he asked with a little annoyance in his voice. "Aren't you feeling well?"

She couldn't bear this.

"Quite," she replied.

His brown eyes became puzzled and angry.

"Have you met anybody?" he asked.

"Nobody who knows me," she said.

"Something has upset you, hasn't it?"

"No, why?" she said, coolly. He did not exist for her except as an annoyance.

His anger grew, filling his throat.

"It seems like it," he said, making an effort not to show his anger, because there seemed no reason for it. He went away downstairs. She sat still on the bed, almost empty. The time went by. She could smell the lunch being served, the smoke of her husband's pipe from the garden. But she could not move. And then he climbed the stairs again. At every step her heart grew tight in her. He opened the door.

"Lunch is on the table," he said.

It was difficult for her to bear him, because he wouldn't leave her alone. She rose stiffly and went down. She could neither eat nor talk during the meal. She sat empty, torn, without a life of her own. He tried to go on as if nothing were the matter. But at last he became silent with anger. As soon as it was possible, she went upstairs again, and locked the bedroom door. She must be alone. He went with his pipe into the garden. All his dark anger burst against her. He had never really won her, she had never loved him. He was only a worker in the mines, she was above him. The pain worked in his soul and now all his anger came up against her.

He turned and went indoors. The third time, she heard him climbing the stairs. Her heart stood still. He pushed the door – it was locked. He tried it again, harder.

"Wait a minute," she said, afraid he would burst the door open.

"What's the matter?" he asked determinedly.

He made her feel sick. She couldn't bear even to look at him.

"Can't you leave me alone?" she replied, turning her face from him.

"I want to know," he said. His face was grey, pale, ugly.

She lifted her head, quickly, like a thing that tries to get free. She looked at him. Her eyes were cold.

"You know I used to live here?" she began in a hard voice, as if to hurt him. He nodded. There was a pause.

"I met an officer. He was fond of me, and I was fond of him – very."

Her husband stood motionless, watching her movements which filled his blood with anger.

"How old was he?" asked the husband.

"When I first knew him, he was twenty-six, nearly three years older –"

"And what then?" asked her husband.

"And then he went away – to fight – in Africa, and almost the first day I met you I heard he was dead."

"He left you?" said the husband, wanting to hurt her, to force himself back into her mind.

"Yes," she said to anger him.

"So you've been going to all your old places!" he said. "That's why you wanted to go out by yourself this morning."

There was a long silence of hate and suffering.

"And how far did it go between you?" he asked at last, in a frightened, stiff voice.

"We loved each other," she cried, "and we *were* lovers – we were. I don't care what *you* think: what have you got to do with it? We were lovers before ever I knew you –"

He shrank, and became white, impersonal. There was a long, dead silence. He seemed to have gone small.

"You never thought to tell me all this before I married you," he said, bitterly, at last.

"You never asked me," she replied.

Suddenly she added:

"And I saw him today," she said. "He is not dead, he's mad."

Her husband looked at her, shocked.

"Mad!" he said.

"Mad," she said. It almost made her feel mad to say the word. There was a pause.

"Did he know you?" asked the husband, in a small voice.

"No," she said.

He stood and looked at her. At last he had learned the width of the gap between them. She still sat on the bed. He couldn't go near her. They couldn't touch each other. The thing must work itself out. They were both shocked so much, they were impersonal, and no longer hated each other. After some minutes he left her and went out.

Odour of Chrysanthemums

*In this story, written in 1909, Lawrence writes about a
world he knew well, the world of small mining villages in the
English Midlands. Here, the struggle between husband and wife
becomes unimportant in the face of the danger and poverty that
were part of the everyday life of the miner. The world shown is
full of darkness lit only by the unnatural flames of the chimneys.
Nature is defeated by the blackness of industrial England.*

THE SMALL TRAIN, NUMBER 4, appeared slowly, noisily
around the corner with seven full trucks of coal.
Elizabeth Bates, walking up the railway line to
home, drew back into the hedge, held her basket aside and
watched. She stood trapped between the black trucks of the
passing train and the hedge. The smoke from the engine
sank into the rough grass.

The fields looked grey and empty. Even the birds seemed
to have left the small lake to nest somewhere else. The
chimneys of the mine rose beyond the lake and the flames
were like red sores in the dead light of the afternoon. The
two wheels were spinning fast up against the sky. The
miners were coming up.

Miners, single and in groups, passed like shadows going
home. At the edge of the railway track, there was a low
miner's cottage. In the long garden there were a few, miserable flowers and vegetables. Elizabeth walked up the path
where pink chrysanthemums hung untidily like pink cloths
on the bushes.

She was a tall, good-looking woman. Her smooth black
hair was parted exactly. For a few moments she stood
steadily watching the miners as they passed along the
railway. Her face was calm and set. Her mouth was closed

25

with disappointment.

After a moment she called:

"John!"

There was no answer. She waited, and then said clearly: "Where are you?"

"Here!" replied a child's voice from the bushes.

"Come in, come on in," she said, "it's getting dark."

The boy advanced slowly and unwillingly. He was dressed in trousers of a cloth that was thick and hard. They had clearly been made from a man's trousers. As he went slowly towards the house he tore at the chrysanthemums and dropped them in handfuls along the path.

"Don't do that — it looks nasty," said his mother. He stopped and she, suddenly pitiful, broke off a flower and held it against her face. When mother and son reached the door her hand hesitated and, instead of laying the flower aside, she pushed it into her belt. The mother and son looked across at the miners going home.

The noise of a small train came closer. Suddenly the engine appeared and stopped opposite. The engine driver, a short man with a round grey beard, leaned out.

"Have you got a cup of tea?" he said in a cheerful, hearty fashion.

It was her father. The woman went into the house and returned with a cup of tea and a piece of bread and butter.

"You needn't have brought me bread and butter," said the father. He drank for a moment or two.

"I heard that Walter's been drinking again," he said.

"When hasn't he?" said the woman bitterly.

"I heard that he was drunk in the Lord Nelson pub and that he was spending a lot of money on Saturday night."

"Very likely," she laughed bitterly. "He only gives me twenty-three shillings."

"It's a bad thing when a man can do nothing with his money but make a beast of himself!" said the grey-bearded man. The woman turned her head away. Her father swallowed the last of the tea and handed her the cup.

The little engine groaned and the train moved slowly

away. The woman looked across the line. Darkness was falling. Miners in grey groups were still passing home. Elizabeth Bates looked at the flow of men, then she went indoors. Her husband did not come.

The kitchen was small and full of firelight; red coals shone in the mouth of the chimney. The cloth was laid for tea; the cups were white in the shadows. The boy sat in the back of the room playing. His interest in himself reminded her of her husband. Her husband seemed to occupy her mind. He had probably gone past his home, slid past his own door, to drink before he came in, while his dinner spoiled and wasted. She glanced at the clock, then went to the door. The garden and the fields were closed in uncertain darkness. She saw that the yellow lamps were lit along the road. Then again she watched the men going home, fewer now and fewer.

Indoors the fire was sinking and the room was dark red. Suddenly, quick young steps came to the door. A little girl entered and began pulling off her outdoor things, dragging a mass of gold and brown curls over her eyes with her hat. Her mother said that she would have to keep her at home in the dark winter days if she was going to come home late from school.

"Why, mother, it's hardly dark yet. The lamp's not lit and my father's not home," Annie said.

No, he isn't. But it's a quarter to five! Did you see anything of him?" The child became serious. She looked at her mother with large, blue eyes. "No, mother, I haven't seen him."

He's probably sitting in the pub," said the mother bitterly.

They sat down to tea. John, at the end of the table near the door, was almost lost in the darkness. Their faces were hidden from each other. Soon the room was busy with the sound of eating. The mother ate very little. She drank her tea and sat thinking.

Suddenly she said angrily, "It's a terrible thing when a man can't even come home to his dinner. He goes past his own door to a pub and I sit here with his dinner waiting for him –"

As she dropped piece after piece of coal on the red fire, the shadows fell on the walls, till the room was almost in total darkness.

"I can't see," complained John.

In spite of herself, the mother laughed.

"You know the way to your mouth," she said. "You're as bad as your father when it gets a bit dark."

Nevertheless, she lit the lamp that hung in the middle of the room.

"Oh, mother!" said Annie. "You've got a flower in your belt. Let me smell," said the child, coming forward and putting her face to the mother's waist. She put the pale chrysanthemums to her lips, murmuring "Don't they smell beautiful!"

Her mother gave a short laugh. "No," she said "not to me. It was chrysanthemums when I married him, and chrysanthemums when you were born, and the first time they ever brought him home drunk, he'd got brown chrysanthemums in his buttonhole."

She looked at the children. Their eyes and their parted lips were wondering. The mother sat in silence for some time. Then she looked at the clock.

"Twenty minutes to six! He won't come home now till they bring him home, rolling in his dirt. *I* won't wash him. He can lie on the floor – Ah, what a fool I've been, what a fool! And this is what I came here for, to this dirty hole!"

The children played together for an hour or more, united in fear of their mother's anger and their father's return. Mrs Bates sat in her chair sewing with energy, listening to the children. Her anger wearied itself, lay down to rest, opening its eyes from time to time and raising its ears to listen. Sometimes, she heard footsteps outside and she would tell the children to be quiet but the footsteps went past the gate. The room was silent, waiting for something to happen.

"It's time for bed," said the mother.

"My father hasn't come," cried Annie.

28

"Never mind. They'll bring him home when he does come – like a log." She meant that there wouldn't be any disturbance. "And he can sleep on the floor till he wakes himself. I know he won't go to work tomorrow after this!"

The children had their hands and faces wiped. They were very quiet. When they had put on their pyjamas, they said their prayers. The mother looked down at them, at the girl's brown curls and the boy's black hair, and her heart burst with anger at their father who caused all three such pain. The children hid their faces in her skirts for comfort.

When Mrs Bates came down, the room was strangely empty. She picked up her sewing and worked for some time without raising her head. Meanwhile her anger was mixed with fear.

II

The clock struck eight and she rose suddenly, dropping her sewing in her chair. She went to the door, opened it, listening. Then she went out, locking the door behind her.

Something moved in the dark and she jumped, though she knew it was only one of the many rats in the place. The night was very dark. She could only see a few yellow lamps and the burning red of the mine chimneys. She hurried along the edge of the railway track and came to the main road. Then her fear faded. People were walking; she saw lights in the houses. Further on were the broad windows of The Prince of Wales pub, very warm and bright, and she could hear the loud voices of the men. What a fool she had been to imagine that anything had happened to him! He was just drinking over there in the pub. She didn't want to go in to bring him out. So she continued her walk towards a long line of houses.

She came to a passage between the houses and called the name of Mrs Rigley. A woman leaned out of a kitchen window.

"Mrs Bates?" she asked.

"Yes, I wondered if your husband was at home. Mine hasn't come yet."

"Hasn't he! Jack's been home, had his dinner and gone to the pub for half an hour. Did you call at The Prince of Wales?"

"No, I didn't like to. I expect he's stuck in there!" Elizabeth Bates said bitterly.

"Come in for a minute. I'll go and ask Jack if he knows anything," said Mrs Rigley.

Elizabeth Bates stepped inside. The other woman apologised for the state of the room and hurried out. Elizabeth sat there looking at the general untidiness of the room. Then she counted the shoes of various sizes scattered over the floor. She sighed and said to herself, "No wonder!"

Two pairs of feet scratched outside the door and the Rigleys entered. Rigley was a big man with very large bones. Across his forehead was a blue scar caused by a wound got in the mines, a wound which the coal dust had turned blue.

"Hasn't he come home yet?" asked the man with sympathy. "I couldn't say where he is – he's not in The Prince of Wales."

"Perhaps he's gone to The Yew Tree pub," said Mrs Rigley.

There was another pause. Rigley clearly had something worrying him. "I left him finishing some work," he began. "He said he would just be a minute, so I came up, thinking he would be just behind me." He stood troubled, as if accused of wrongly leaving his friend.

Elizabeth Bates, now again full of fear, hurried to calm him.

"Don't worry. I expect he's gone up to The Yew Tree as you say. It's not the first time I've worried myself into a fever. He'll come home when they carry him."

"I'll just go and make sure that he's there," said Mr Rigley, afraid of frightening Mrs Bates.

"Oh, I wouldn't think of worrying you that far," said Elizabeth Bates, but he knew she was glad of his offer.

She walked quickly back to her cottage. The room was quiet. Mrs Bates took off her hat and sat down. It was a few minutes past nine. She jumped at the sound of the winding-engine at the mine and the sharp grinding of the ropes as it descended. Again she felt the painful sweep of her blood, and she put her hand to her side, saying aloud, "It's only the manager going down to make his regular check."

She sat still, listening. Half an hour of this and she was wearied out.

"What am I working myself up like this for?" she said pitiably to herself. "I'll only be doing myself some damage."

She took out her sewing again.

At a quarter to ten there were footsteps. One person! She watched for the door to open. It was an elderly woman in black, about sixty years old, pale with blue eyes, and her face deeply lined with sadness. She shut the door and turned to her daughter-in-law:

"Ah, whatever shall we do, whatever shall we do!" she cried.

Elizabeth drew back a little, sharply.

"What is it mother?" she said.

"I don't know, child. I can't tell you. There's no end to my troubles, there isn't!" She cried without wiping her eyes, the tears running.

"But, mother," interrupted Elizabeth, "what do you mean? What is it?"

The grandmother slowly wiped her eyes.

"Poor child! Ah, you poor thing!"

Elizabeth waited.

"Is he dead?" she asked, and at the words her heart swung violently.

"Don't say so, Elizabeth! We'll hope it's not as bad as that. May the Lord spare us that! Mr Rigley came and told me to come and wait with you and they'd bring him home."

The old woman continued to cry and complain but Elizabeth's thoughts were elsewhere. If he was killed, would she be able to manage on the little money she would have? If he was hurt, how awkward he would be to nurse! But

31

perhaps she'd be able to get him away from the drink and his hateful ways. She would – while he was ill. The tears offered to come to her eyes at the picture. But she turned to consider the children. She was absolutely necessary for them. They were her business.

"Yes!" repeated the old woman, "he was a good man, Elizabeth, he was, in his way. I don't know why he got to be such trouble, I don't. He was happy at home, only full of spirits. I hope the Lord will spare him to mend his ways. I hope so. I hope so. I don't know how it is . . ."

The old woman continued to think aloud, a dull annoying sound. Elizabeth thought hard and jumped once when she heard the engines at the mine scream and then slow and then make no sound. The woman did not notice. Elizabeth waited for something to happen. The mother-in-law talked, and sometimes fell silent.

It was half past ten. The old woman was saying: "But it's trouble from beginning to end; you're never too old for trouble, never too old for that – " when the gate shut noisily and there were heavy feet on the steps.

"I'll go, let me go," cried the old woman. But Elizabeth was at the door. It was a man from the mines.

"They're bringing him in," he said.

Elizabeth's heart stopped for a moment.

"Is he – is it bad?" she asked.

The man turned away, looking at the darkness. "The doctor says he's been dead for hours."

The old woman who stood just behind Elizabeth dropped into a chair crying: "Oh, my boy, my boy!"

"Quiet!" said Elizabeth sharply. "Be still, mother, don't wake the children."

The old woman cried softly. The man moved back. Elizabeth took a step forward.

"How did it happen?" she asked.

"I couldn't say for sure," the man replied, uneasily. "He was finishing his work and a lot of stuff came down behind him. It shut him in and he couldn't breathe."

Elizabeth heard the old woman cry aloud behind her.

"Oh, mother," she said, putting her hand on the old woman, "don't wake the children, don't wake the children."

She cried a little unknowingly while the old mother groaned to herself. Elizabeth remembered that they were bringing him home, and she must be ready. "They'll lay him in the front room," she said to herself, standing a moment, pale and confused.

Then she lighted a candle and went into the small room. The air was cold and damp but she couldn't make a fire there, there was no fireplace. She set down the candle and looked around. The candlelight shone on two jars of pink chrysanthemums. There was a cold deathly smell of chrysanthemums in the room. Elizabeth began to make room for the body.

She went into the kitchen for another candle and there she heard them coming. She stood in the doorway, listening. She heard them pass the end of the house, and come awkwardly down the three steps.

Then Elizabeth heard the manager of the mine say: "You go in first, Jim. Careful!"

The door came open, and the two women saw a miner backing into the room, holding one end of a stretcher, on which they could see the boots of the dead man.

"Where will you have him?" asked the manager, a short, white-bearded man.

"In the front room," she said.

The coat with which they had covered the body fell off as they awkwardly turned in the small room, and the women saw their man, bare to the waist, lying stripped for work. The old woman began to groan in a low voice of horror.

"Lay the stretcher at the side," said the manager, "Be careful, careful, now!"

One of the men had knocked over a jar of chrysanthemums. He stared awkwardly, then they put down the stretcher. Elizabeth did not look at her husband. As soon as she could get in the room, she went and picked up the broken jar and the flowers. The men waited while she cleared up the water.

33

The manager rubbed his head. "I never knew such a thing in my life. He shouldn't have been there. He was shut in but he was hardly touched." He looked down at the dead man, lying half-bare, covered in coal-dust. The miners looked aside hopelessly. The horror of the thing touched them all.

Then they heard the girl's voice upstairs calling:

"Mother, mother – who is it? Mother, who is it?"

Elizabeth hurried to the foot of the stairs and opened the door:

"Go to sleep!" she commanded sharply. "What are you shouting about? Go to sleep at once – there's nothing –"

Then she began to climb the stairs. They could hear her on the floor of the little bedroom. They could hear her clearly:

"What's the matter now?–what's the matter with you, silly thing?" – her voice was shaking with an unreal gentleness.

"I thought some men came," said the voice of the child. "Has he come?"

"Yes, they've brought him. Go to sleep now, like a good child."

They could hear her voice in the bedroom.

"Is he drunk?" asked the girl faintly.

"No! No – he's not! He – he's asleep."

"Is he asleep downstairs?"

"Yes – and don't make a noise."

There was silence for a moment, then the men heard the frightened child again:

"What's that noise?"

"It's nothing, I tell you, what are you worrying about?"

The noise was the grandmother groaning. The manager put his hand on her arm and signalled to the men to leave. None of them spoke until they were far from the house.

When Elizabeth came down she found the mother alone, leaning over the dead man, the tears dropping on him.

"We must wash him," the wife said. She put water on to boil and then bent to untie his boots. The room was damp and dark with only one candle. At last she got off the heavy boots and put them away.

"You must help me now," she whispered to the old woman. Together they undressed the man.

They saw him in the simple state of death. The women stood in fear and respect. For a few moments they remained still, looking down, the old woman weeping. Elizabeth felt defeated. He lay complete in himself. She had nothing to do with him. She could not accept it. Bending, she laid her hand on him, to claim him. He was still warm, for the mine was hot where he had died. His mother had his face between her hands and her old tears fell like drops from wet leaves. Elizabeth touched the body of her husband with her lips. She seemed to be listening, trying to get some connection. But she could not. She was driven away. He could not be touched.

She went into the kitchen, where she poured warm water into a bowl, brought soap and a soft towel.

"I must wash him," she said.

Then the old mother watched Elizabeth as she carefully washed his face, carefully brushing the big moustache from his mouth. She was afraid with a deep fear, so she cared for him.

The old woman, jealous, said: "Let me wipe him!"

She wiped as Elizabeth washed. They worked thus in silence for a long time. They never forgot it was death. At last it was finished. He was a man of powerful body, and his face showed no signs of drink. He was full-fleshed with a fine, firm body. But he was dead.

"Bless him," whispered his mother looking always at his face in terror.

Elizabeth sank down again to the floor, and put her face against his neck. But she had to draw away again. He was dead and her living flesh had no place against his.

The man's mouth was slightly open under the moustache. The eyes, half-shut, were in shadow. Burning life had gone from him and had left him apart from her. And she knew what a stranger he was to her. She knew that she had never

35

seen him. He had never seen her. They had met in the dark and had fought in the dark. And now she saw and was silent.

In fear and shame she looked at this body. And he was the father of her children. It seemed terrible to her. She looked at his face and she turned her own face to the wall.

And her heart was bursting with grief and pity for him. What had he suffered? She had not been able to help him. He had been cruelly hurt and she could not give him anything back. There were the children – but the children belonged to life. This dead man had nothing to do with them. The children had come, for some mysterious reason, out of both of them. Now he was dead. She saw this part of her life closed. It was finished then. It had become hopeless between them long before he died. Yet he had been her husband. But how little!

"Have you got his shirt, Elizabeth?"

"It's ready," she said.

It was hard work to dress him. He was so heavy and still. A terrible fear was in her: he was so heavy and completely still, unmoving, apart. The horror of the distance between them was almost too much for her.

At last it was finished. They covered him with a sheet. And she closed the door of the little front room so that the children wouldn't see what was lying there. Then, with peace sunk heavy on her heart, she began to tidy the kitchen. She knew that she yielded to life, her immediate master. But in the face of death, her last master, she trembled with fear and shame.

The Prussian Officer

*This story was written in 1913. On the surface, the
story is about a cruel officer and a helpless servant but there are
strange feelings beneath that relationship. At times, the reader can
see how the cruelty of the officer comes from a feeling of jealousy
that is almost sexual. In the violent reaction of the young servant,
Lawrence uses language that could be used to describe love-making
The feelings of the characters in this story are not very far away
from those in the first two stories. It is about power and the
narrow line that separates terrible hate from love.*

THEY HAD MARCHED MORE THAN TWENTY MILES since early
morning along the white hot road where occasional
trees threw a moment of shade, then out into the sun
again. The valley, wide and shallow, burnt with heat. But
right in front were the mountains, pale blue and very still,
snow shining gently on them. And towards the mountains,
on and on, the soldiers marched between the fields which
threw off a breathless heat. The feet of the soldiers grew
hotter and sweat ran through their hair.

He walked on and on in silence, staring at the mountains
ahead. He could now walk almost without pain. At the start,
he had determined not to limp. It had made him sick to take
the first steps, and during the first mile or so, he had held
his breath and cold drops of sweat had stood on his forehead.
But he had walked till it no longer troubled him. What were
they after all but bruises! He had looked at them as he was
getting up: deep bruises on the backs of his legs. And since
he had made his first step, he had been conscious of them,
so that now he had a tight, hot place in his chest with
holding the pain in. There seemed no air when he breathed.

He saw the fine figure of the officer on horseback ahead

in a pale blue uniform with deep red markings. The sun flashed on the metal of the officer's sword and the dark sweat shone on his silky brown horse. He was the officer's servant and he felt connected with that figure. He followed it like a shadow, silent and trapped and cursed by it. And the officer was always conscious of the soldiers behind him, and of his servant among them.

The officer was a tall man of about forty, grey at the forehead. He was a fine figure and one of the best horsemen in the West. His servant admired the strength of his leg muscles when he had to rub him down.

For the rest, the servant hardly noticed the officer any more than he noticed himself. He did not often look at his master's face. The officer had reddish-brown, stiff hair that he wore short. His face was strong, lined and thin, and there was an anger in him which gave him the look of a man who fights with life. His light blue eyes flashed with cold fire.

He was a Prussian of high birth, proud and inhuman. He had never married. He spent his time on horseback and at the officers' club. Now and then he had a woman but he returned to duty still more unsatisfied and angry. With the men, however, he was merely impersonal though a devil when he lost his temper. On the whole, they feared him but did not hate him. They accepted him because they had no choice.

At first he was cold but fair to his servant. So his servant knew almost nothing about him except what orders he would give and how he wanted them obeyed. That was quite simple. Then the change gradually came.

The servant was about twenty-two years old, of average height, and well-built. He had a strong, heavy body and a soft, black, young moustache. His eyes were dark, expressionless, as if he never thought but only received life through his senses, and acted straight from instinct.

Gradually the officer became conscious of the servant's young energy and strength. He could not get away from it. It was like a warm flame upon the older man's stiff body. And this made the Prussian angry. He could easily have changed this man, but he didn't. He now rarely looked at his servant but he would notice the strong, young shoulders under the blue cloth, the bend of his neck. When he saw the young brown hand grasp a loaf or a wine bottle, a flash of hate or anger went through the older man's blood. It was not because the youth was awkward. It was the instinctive sureness of a free young animal that drove the officer to such fury.

Once, when a bottle of wine had gone over and the red spilt out on to the tablecloth, the officer had jumped up with a curse and his eyes, blue like fire, had confused and shocked the young soldier. He felt something sink, deeper and deeper into his soul, where nothing had gone before. It left him empty and wondering. Some confidence in himself was gone, a little anxiety had taken its place. And from that time on an undiscovered feeling had held between the two men.

The servant was afraid of really meeting his master. He remembered the steel-blue eyes and didn't intend to meet them again. So he always stared past his master, and avoided him. Also, in a little anxiety, he waited for the three months to go when he could leave the army.

He had served the officer for more than a year, and knew his duty. He performed it easily, as if it were natural to him. He took the officer and his commands as he took the sun and the rain. It was unavoidable. But now if he were forced into personal relations with his master, he would be like a wild thing, caught. He felt that he must get away.

The young soldier seemed to live naturally and freely like a wild animal and this cut through the officer's stiff sense of discipline. In spite of himself, the officer couldn't keep his professional distance from the man nor could he leave him alone. In spite of himself, he watched him, gave him sharp orders, tried to take up as much of his time as possible. Sometimes he flew into a fury and then the servant shut himself off and waited for the end of the noise. The words never reached his intelligence.

The officer knew that his servant would soon be free, and

would be glad. He grew madly angry. He couldn't rest when the soldier was away, and when he was present, he stared at him with furious, pained eyes. And he became cruel. The young soldier only grew more silent and expressionless.

"What cattle were you born from that you can't keep straight eyes? Look at me when I speak to you."

And the soldier turned his dark eyes but there was no sight in them.

Once the officer threw a heavy army glove into the young man's face. Then he had the satisfaction of seeing the black eyes burn into his own, like straw thrown into a fire. And he laughed – scornfully.

But there were only two months more. The young man tried to keep himself together. All his instinct was to avoid personal feeling, even hate. But in spite of himself the hate grew. The officer seemed to be going mad, and the young man was deeply frightened.

The soldier had a girlfriend, a girl from the mountains, simple and independent. The two walked together, rather silently. He went with her, not to talk, but to have his arm round her, and for the comfort of her touch. This made it easier for him to forget the officer; for he could rest with her and hold her tight against his chest. And she, in some silent fashion, was there for him. They loved each other.

The officer knew it and was mad with anger. He kept the young man busy every evening and enjoyed the dark look that came on his face.

The officer tried hard not to admit to the madness of the feelings that had come over him. He pretended that they were just those of a man made angry by a stupid servant. His nerves, however, were suffering. At last, he hit the servant in the face with the end of a belt. When he saw the pain and tears in the young man's eyes and the blood on his mouth, he had felt a deep pleasure and shame.

But this, he admitted to himself, was a thing he had never done before. His own nerves must be falling apart. He went away for some days with a woman but it was no pleasure.

He came back in anger and misery and ordered supper.

The meal went on in silence but the servant seemed eager to get it over.

"Are you in a hurry?" asked the officer, watching the warm face of his servant. There was no reply.

"Will you answer my question?" said the officer.

"Yes, sir," came the answer that sent a flash through the listener.

"For what?"

"I was going out, sir."

"I want you this evening."

"Yes, sir," replied the servant, in his throat.

"I want you tomorrow evening also – in fact I want you every evening from now on unless I tell you otherwise."

The mouth with the young moustache closed.

"Yes, sir," answered the servant, loosening his lips for a moment.

He turned to the door.

"And why do you have a piece of pencil behind your ear?"

The servant took the pencil and put it in his pocket without answering. He had been copying some poetry for his girlfriend's birthday card. He returned to finish clearing the table. His master was standing near the stove with a little eager smile on his face.

"Why do you have a piece of pencil behind your ear?" he asked.

The young soldier's heart suddenly ran hot. He felt blind. Instead of answering he turned to the door. As he bent to put down the dishes, he was knocked down by a kick from behind.

And as he was rising he was kicked heavily again and again.

The officer's heart ached, almost with pleasure, as he saw the young man get to his feet uncertainly and with pain.

"I asked you a question."

"Yes, sir."

"Why did you have a pencil behind your ear?"

Again the servant's heart ran hot and he couldn't breathe. A smile came into the officer's eyes and he lifted his foot.

41

"I – I – forgot it – sir."

"What was it doing there?"

"I had been writing."

"Writing what?"

Again the soldier looked at him without reply. The officer could hear him trying to breathe. The smile came into the blue eyes. The soldier worked his dry throat but couldn't speak. Suddenly the smile lit like a flame and a kick came heavily against the servant's leg. His face went dead with two black, staring eyes.

"Well?" said the officer.

"Some poetry, sir," came the broken, unrecognisable voice.

"Poetry, what poetry?" asked the officer, with a little smile.

Again there was the working in the throat. The officer's heart had suddenly gone down heavily, and he stood sick and tired.

"For my girl, sir," he heard the dry inhuman sound.

"Oh!" he said, turning away. "Clear the table."

"Yes, sir."

The young soldier was gone, looking old, and walking heavily.

The officer, left alone, held himself stiffly. His instinct warned him that he must not think. Deep inside him was the violent joy of his anger, still working powerfully. Then there was another feeling, a horrible breaking down of something. And he drank himself into unconsciousness. When he woke in the morning, he was deeply shaken. And when his servant appeared with coffee, he refused to remember the event of the night before. He had not done any such thing – not he.

The servant had gone about as if in a dream all evening. He drank some beer because he was thirsty, but not much, the alcohol made his feeling come back, and he could not bear it. His mouth hung slightly open, like a fool's. He felt empty and wasted. But he was very tired. He got to bed at last, and slept unmoving, a dead night with flashes of pain.

There was the march in the morning. But he woke early. The painful ache in his chest, the dryness of his throat, the terrible feeling of misery made his eyes feel dull the moment he woke. The last bit of darkness was being pushed out of the room. He only wished it would stay night, so that he could lie still, covered by darkness. And yet nothing would prevent the day from coming, nothing would save him from having to get up. He must go and take the coffee to the officer.

At last he got up. He felt lost, confused and helpless. Then he grasped the bed, the pain was so fierce. And looking at his legs, he saw the darker bruises and knew that, if he pressed one of his fingers on one of the bruises, he would faint. But he didn't want to faint – he didn't want anybody to know. It was between him and the officer. There were only two people in the world now – himself and the officer.

Slowly, he got dressed and forced himself to walk. He took the coffee and went to the officer's room. The officer, pale and heavy, sat at the table; his hand trembled as he drank the coffee. The soldier felt dead, out of the world. And he went away, feeling as if he were coming to pieces. And when the officer was there on horseback, giving orders, while he stood sick with pain, he felt as if he must shut his eyes – on everything. It was only the long pain of marching with a dry throat that filled him with one single, sleep-heavy intention: to save himself.

II

He was getting used even to his dry throat. He marched on uncomplaining. He did not want to speak, not to anybody. The scent of the fields drowned in sunshine came like a sickness. And the march continued, endlessly, like a bad sleep.

At the next farmhouse there was water. The soldiers gathered round to drink. The officer sat on horseback watching. There was a dark shadow over his light, fierce eyes. The servant had to move past the figure of the horseman. It was not that he was afraid. It was as if he were an empty shell. He felt himself to be nothing, a shadow creeping under the sunshine. And, although he was thirsty, he could scarcely drink, feeling the officer near him. He wanted to stay in the shadow, not to be forced into consciousness.

The soldiers moved slowly up the burning hillside. Sometimes it was dark before the young man's eyes, as if he saw his world through smoked glass, shadowy and unreal. It gave him a pain in his head to walk.

At last, they stopped to rest. The soldiers were steaming with heat, but they were lively. He sat still, seeing the blue mountains rising above the land, about fifteen miles away. At the foot, there was the broad, pale bed of the river. Nearer, a red-roofed cottage with a white base and square dots of windows. There were long strips of grass and pale green corn. And just at his feet, a dark muddy field where a few pale gold flowers burst. He thought he was going to sleep.

Suddenly something moved before his eyes. The officer, a small, light blue and red figure, was moving evenly between the strips of corn. The horseman's figure was proud and sure, a quick bright thing which caught all the light of the morning. The young soldier sat and stared. But as the horse slowed to a walk, the great flash burned over the body and soul of the servant.

The officer looked at the soldiers scattered on the hillside. The scene pleased him. And he was feeling proud. His servant was among them, under his control.

The young soldier's heart was like fire in his chest. Then the officer called him. The flame leapt into the young soldier's throat as he heard the command, and he rose blindly. He did not look up. But the officer's voice trembled slightly.

"Go to the inn and fetch me some beer ..." The officer gave his commands. "Quick!" he added.

At the last word, the heart of the servant leapt with a flash, but he turned in mechanical obedience and ran

44

heavily downhill. It was only the outside of his body that was obeying so humbly and mechanically. Inside, all the energy of that young life had gathered. He collected the beer and walked quickly back uphill. There was a pain in his head but, in the centre of his chest, he was firm, not to be pulled to pieces.

The officer had gone up into the wood. The servant approached the green entrance. There in the half-shade, he saw the horse standing, the sunshine and the shadow of leaves dancing over its brown body. A hot flash passed through the soldier's stomach as he walked heavily towards his officer.

The officer watched the young soldier approach and his blood, too, ran hot. This was to be man-to-man between them. The officer watched the sunburned hands of the soldier open a bottle.

"Hot!" he said, as if friendly.

"Yes, sir," the soldier replied between shut teeth.

And he heard the sound of the officer's drinking. He watched the white hand that grasped the bottle. It was raised. He followed it with his eyes. And then he saw the thin, strong throat moving up and down, the strong jaw working. And the instinct which had been pulling at the young man's wrist suddenly burst free. He jumped, feeling as if he were torn in two by a strong flame.

The officer's foot caught in the root of a tree. He went backwards with a crash. And in a second, the servant, with serious, earnest young face, had got his knee in the officer's chest and he was pressing the head backwards, pressing, with all his heart. He felt relief at the ache in his wrists. And with his hands, he pushed at the face, with all his strength. And it was pleasant, too, to have that face, that hard jaw already slightly rough with beard, in his hands. He did not rest for a moment, but, with all the force of his joyous blood, he pushed till he felt the neck break. The officer's body shook heavily, frightening and horrifying the young soldier. Yet it pleased him too. It pleased him to keep his hands pressing the jaw back, to feel the chest of the

45

other man give under the weight of his strong young knees, to feel the trembling of the body shaking his own, which was pressed down on it.

But it went still. The head hung backwards. He could look into the nose of the other man, the eyes he could hardly see. How strangely the mouth was pushed out. Then he noticed that the nose gradually filled with blood. The red hesitated, ran over, and went in a thin stream down the face to the eyes.

It shocked and upset him. He stood and looked at the unmoving body in silence. He was afraid to look at the eyes. They were horrible now – only the whites showing, and the blood running to them. Well it was done. In his heart he was satisfied. He had hated the face of the officer but he could not bear to see the long, military body lying broken. He wanted to hide it away.

Quickly, busily he pushed it under a pile of logs. He sat by it for a few moments. Here his own life also ended.

He knew he must go. He stood up. It surprised him that the leaves were shining in the sun. For him the world had changed. But for the rest it had not – all seemed the same. Only he had left it. And he could not go back.

He saw the horse standing in the path. He got on and rode deep into the wood. There it was dark and cool. And he was sick with pain. Trying to get down from the horse, he fell, astonished at the pain and his lack of balance. The horse moved uneasily. He hit its side and sent it racing away. It was his last connection with life as he had known it.

He only wanted to lie down and not be disturbed, but as soon as he closed his eyes, his consciousness went racing on without him. His sickness beat in him as if it beat through the whole earth. He was burning with dry heat. But he was too busy, too active in his screaming brain, to notice.

III

He woke suddenly. His mouth was dry and hard, his heart beat heavily, but he hadn't the energy to get up. Where was he? There was something knocking. He struggled to consciousness. And gradually he knew his surroundings. Somebody was knocking. Then everything went black. Yet he didn't believe he had closed his eyes. Out of the blackness, sight slowly came back again. He saw the blood-covered face of the officer, which he hated. And he held himself still with horror. Someone was knocking. He lay absolutely still, as if dead with fear. And he went unconscious.

When he opened his eyes again he saw something creeping quickly up the tree. It was a little bird. And the bird was whistling overhead. Tap – tap – tap – it was the small quick bird knocking on the tree. How neat it was. There were several of them. They were so pretty – but they crept like mice, running here and there among the leaves.

He lay down again. He had a horror of little creeping birds. All his blood seemed to be creeping in his head. And yet he could not move.

He awoke with a further ache of weariness. There was the pain in his head, and the horrible sickness, and his inability to move. He had got beyond himself. He had never been here before. Was it life, or not life? He was by himself. There had been father and mother and lover. What did they all matter? This was the open land.

He struggled to his feet. He went on walking, walking, looking for something – for a drink. His brain felt hot for lack of water. He went on, unconscious as he walked, his mouth open. And the fever went on inside him – his brain opening and shutting like the night. The world hung around him for moments, fields in the grey-green light, and the clouds black across the sky. Then the darkness fell and the night was complete.

In the morning he came definitely awake. Then his brain flamed with the horror of his thirstiness. The sun was on his face and steam rose from his wet clothes. He got up. There, straight in front of him, blue and cool and tender, were the mountains clear against the pale edge of the morning sky. He wanted them – he wanted them alone –

he wanted to leave himself and be joined with them. They were still and soft with white gentle markings of snow. He stood still, mad with suffering, his hands trembling and grasping. Then he was twisting hopelessly in the grass.

He lay in a kind of dream of pain. His thirst seemed separate from him. The pain he felt was another self. He was moving away from it. The sun burning down on him was breaking the connection between them. He stared at the shining mountains. There they stood, all still and wonderful between earth and heaven. He stared till his eyes went black, and the mountains, as they stood in their beauty, so clean and cool, seemed to have that which was lost in him.

IV

When the soldiers found him, three hours later, he was lying with his face over his arm, his black hair giving off heat under the sun. But he was still alive. Seeing the open black mouth, the young soldiers dropped him in horror.

He died in hospital at night, without having seen again. The doctors saw the bruises on his legs and were silent.

The bodies of the two men lay together, side by side, the one white and stiff, the other looking as if at any moment it would awake, so young and unused, from its rest.

The Horse Dealer's Daughter

This story was written in 1916 and it looks at the mysterious power of love in relation to class and death. But this is not, though, the story of a usual love affair. There are none of the scenes that the reader might expect. Instead, love is seen as something that is beyond words, an instinct that rises to the surface even against the desires of one of the characters. Love is not comfortable here. It is a frightening feeling, a little perhaps like drowning.

"WELL, MABEL, AND WHAT ARE YOU GOING TO DO WITH YOURSELF?" asked Joe, with foolish cheerfulness. He felt quite safe himself. Without listening for an answer, he turned away. He didn't care about anything, since he felt safe himself.

The three brothers and the sister sat around the joyless breakfast table, attempting to discuss the problem. The morning post had brought the fatal news, the business would have to close and all was over. The heavy furniture itself looked as if it were waiting to be got rid of.

But the discussion amounted to nothing. The three men sat at the table smoking and thinking about their own condition. The girl was alone, a rather short, unhappy-looking young woman of twenty-seven. She didn't share the same life as her brothers. She would have been good-looking, except for the empty, fixed expression she wore on her face.

There was a confused sound of horses' feet outside. The three men turned to watch. A group were being taken for exercise. This was the last time. These were the last horses that would go through their hands. The young men watched with a critical, unconcerned look. They were all frightened at the falling apart of their lives and this left them no inner freedom.

Yet they were three fine, strong fellows. Joe, the eldest was a man of thirty-three, broad and good-looking in a hot, red-faced way. As he twisted his black moustache over a thick finger, his eyes were shallow and restless. When he laughed, he uncovered his teeth and his manner was stupid. Now he watched the horses with an empty look of helplessness in his eyes.

The great horses swung past. They were tied head to tail, and their great feet sunk into the black mud as they were led round the corner. Every movement showed a massive sleepy strength, and a stupidity which held them in slavery to man.

Joe watched with helpless eyes. The horses were almost like his own body to him. He felt that he was finished now. Luckily, he was to marry a woman as old as himself, and therefore her father, who was manager of a local farm, would give him a job. He would marry and be tied like the horses. His life was over, he would be a working animal now.

Fred Henry, the second brother, was tall, well-built, energetic. He had watched the passing of the horses more calmly. If he was an animal, like Joe, he was an animal which controls, not one which is controlled. He was a master of any horse, and he carried himself with an air of mastery. But he was not master of the situations of life. He pushed his rough brown moustache upwards, off his lip, and glanced as if annoyed at his sister, who sat unmoving and silent.

"You'll go and stay with Lucy for a bit, won't you?" he asked. The girl did not answer.

"I don't see what else you can do," insisted Fred Henry.

"Get a job as a servant," said Joe.

The girl didn't move a muscle.

"If I was her, I'd train to be a nurse," said Malcolm, the youngest of the three. He was the baby of the family, a young man of twenty-two, with a fresh hopeful manner.

But Mabel didn't take any notice of him. They had talked at her and round her for so many years, that she hardly heard them at all.

"Have you had a letter from Lucy?" Fred Henry suddenly asked his sister.

"Last week," came the reply.

"And what does she say?"

There was no answer.

"Did she ask you to go and stay there?" insisted Fred Henry.

"She says I can if I like."

"Well, then, you'd better. Tell her you'll come on Monday."

This was received in silence.

"That's what you'll do then, is it?" said Fred Henry, in some annoyance.

But she made no answer. There was a silence of hopelessness and anger in the room. Malcolm smiled stupidly.

"You'll have to make up your mind between now and next Wednesday," said Joe loudly, "or else you'll find yourself in the streets."

The face of the young woman darkened, but she sat on without expression.

"Here's Jack Fergusson!" exclaimed Malcolm who was looking aimlessly out of the window.

After a moment, a young man entered. He was wearing a thick coat and a cap pulled down on his head. He was of average height, his face was rather long and pale, his eyes looked tired.

"Hello Jack! Well, Jack!" exclaimed Malcolm and Joe. Fred Henry merely said "Jack!"

"What's happening?" asked the newcomer, addressing Fred Henry.

"The same. We've got to be out by Wednesday. Got a cold?"

"I have – and it's a bad one, too," said Jack Fergusson.

"Why don't you stay in?" asked Fred Henry.

"*Me* stay in? When I can't stand on my legs, perhaps I'll

51

have a chance." The young man's voice was rough.

"It doesn't look very good for the patients, does it," said Joe laughing, "if a doctor goes around with a cold."

At this point Mabel rose from the table, and they all seemed to notice her. She began putting the dishes together. The young doctor looked at her, but didn't speak to her. He hadn't greeted her. She went out of the room with the tray, her face unchanging and without expression.

Malcolm and Joe went out after her.

"Well, I shall miss you, Fred," said the young doctor.

"And I'll miss you, Jack," returned the other.

Fred Henry turned aside. There was nothing to say. Mabel came in again to finish clearing the table.

"What are you going to do then, Miss Pervin?" asked Fergusson. "Are you going to your sister's?"

Mabel looked at him with her steady, dangerous eyes, that always made him uncomfortable, unsettling his ease.

"No," she said.

"Well, what *are* you going to do? Say what you *mean* to do?" cried Fred Henry with pointless fury.

But she only turned her head away, and continued her work. Fred Henry spoke angrily under his breath. But she finished her job with a perfectly expressionless face, the young doctor watching her with interest all the time. Then she went out.

Fred Henry stared after her, his lips fixed in fury.

"You can scream at her, but that's all you'll get out of her," he said in a small, narrow voice.

The doctor smiled faintly.

"What is she going to do then?" he asked.

"I don't know!" replied the other.

There was a pause. Then the doctor rose.

"Will I see you tonight?" asked Fred Henry.

"I don't know," said the doctor, "I've got such a cold. But I'll come round to the pub, anyway."

The two young men went through the passage to the back door. The house was large, but grey and empty now. At the back was a big, square yard with stables on two sides.

Sloping, damp, winter-dark fields stretched away on the open sides.

But the stables were empty. Joseph Pervin, the father of the family, had been a man of no education, who had become a fairly large horse dealer. The stables had been full of horses and the kitchen had been full of servants. But recently things had gone bad. The old man was dead and there was nothing but debt and threatening.

For months Mabel had kept the house together, without servants, for her useless brothers. She had always kept house but, before, there had been money. Her brothers had been rough and stupid but, as long as there had been money, the girl had felt herself firmly settled, proud and reserved.

No company came to the house, except for dealers and rough men. Mabel had no friends of her own sex after her sister had gone away. But she didn't mind. She had loved her father and had felt safe with him. Now he had died and left them hopelessly in debt.

She had suffered badly during the time of poverty. But each member of the family kept their strange animal pride. Now, for Mabel, the end had come. Why should she think? Why should she answer anybody? It was enough that this was the end. She needn't worry any more about going into the shops and buying the cheapest food. She thought of nobody, not even of herself. She seemed in a sort of joy to be approaching her dead mother, who was in heaven.

In the afternoon she took a little bag, with some scissors and a small brush, and went out. It was a grey, winter day, with sad, dark-green fields and the air black with smoke from the factories. She went quickly, darkly along the road, noticing nobody, through the town to the churchyard.

There she felt safe, as if no one could see her, although in fact she could be seen by anyone who passed the churchyard wall. Nevertheless, as soon as she was under the shadow of the great church, among the graves, she felt protected from the world, hidden within the thick churchyard walls as if in another country.

Carefully, she began to cut the grass from the grave and wash the stone. It gave her sincere satisfaction to do this. She felt in immediate touch with the world of her mother. Her life here in the world seemed far less real than the world of death that she shared with her mother.

The doctor's house was next door to the church. As he hurried along, Fergusson glanced across the graveyard and saw the girl at her work. She seemed so distant that it was like looking into another world. Something inside him was touched by her. He slowed down as he walked, watching her as if under a spell.

She lifted her eyes, feeling him looking. Their eyes met. And each looked again at once, each feeling, in some way, found out by the other. He lifted his cap in greeting and passed on down the road, but her face stayed with him. There was a heavy power in her eyes which took hold of him. He felt as if he had drunk some strong drug. He had been feeling weak and tired before. Now life came back into him and he felt freed from his daily problems.

He finished his work as quickly as possible. As he started for home, the afternoon was darkening. It was grey, dead, and wintry with a slow, damp, heavy coldness sinking into his soul. But why should he think or notice? He quickly climbed the hill and turned across the dark-green fields, following the black path. In the distance, at the edge of the town, he could see Oldmeadow, the Pervins' house. Well, he wouldn't go there many more times! Another place would be lost to him: the only company he cared for in that ugly little town. There was nothing but work in his life, and it wore him out. But at the same time, it excited his nerves. He could come so near, into the lives of the rough, strongly-feeling people.

Below Oldmeadow, in the green, damp hollow of fields, there was a square, deep pond. The doctor's quick eye noticed a figure in black passing through the gate of the field, down towards the lake. He looked again. It would be Mabel Pervin. His mind suddenly became alive and attentive.

Why was she going down there? He walked up the path and stood staring. His eyes followed her as she moved, direct and determined, as if guided by something, straight down the field towards the lake. There she stood on the bank for a moment. She never raised her head. Then she walked slowly into the water.

He stood motionless as the small black figure walked slowly towards the centre of the lake, very slowly, gradually moving deeper into the motionless water, and still moving forward as the water got up to her breast. Then he could see her no more in the shadow of the dead afternoon.

"There!" he exclaimed. "Would you believe it?"

Then he began to run over the damp field, down into the wintry hollow. It took him several minutes to come to the lake. He stood on the bank, breathing heavily. He could see nothing. He stared into the dead water. Yes, perhaps that was the dark shadow of her black clothing beneath the surface of the water.

He slowly walked into the lake. The bottom was deep and soft, he sank in, and the water grasped dead cold around his legs. As he moved, he could smell the rotten mud that rose up into the water. His lungs were sickened but still he moved deeper into the lake. The cold water rose over his legs, his waist. The lower part of his body was covered in the horrible cold. And the bottom of the pond was so deeply soft and uncertain, he was afraid of falling with his mouth underneath the water. He couldn't swim, and was afraid.

He spread his hands under the water and moved them around, trying to feel for her. The dead cold pond moved against his chest. He walked again, a little deeper, and again, with his hands underneath, he felt all around under the water. And he touched her clothing. But it slipped from his fingers. He made a desperate effort to grasp it.

And doing so he lost his balance and went under, horribly drowning in the muddy water, struggling madly for a few moments. At last, after what seemed hours, his feet touched the bottom and he rose again and looked around. He fought for air, and knew he was in the world. Then he looked at the water. She had risen near him. He grasped her clothing, and pulling her nearer, turned to make his way to land again.

He went very slowly, carefully. He rose higher, climbing out of the lake. The water was now only about his legs; he was thankful, full of relief to escape the grasp of the lake. He lifted her and fell on to the bank, out of the horror of wet, grey mud.

He laid her down. She was quite unconscious and running with water. He made the water come from her mouth, he worked to bring her back to life. He didn't have to work very long before he could feel the breathing begin again in her; she was breathing naturally. He worked a little longer. He could feel her live beneath his hands; she was coming back. He wiped her face, wrapped her in his coat, looked round into the dark-grey world, then lifted her and carried her heavily up the bank and across the fields.

It seemed an impossibly long way, and she felt so heavy that he thought he would never get to her house. But at last, he was there. He opened the door and went in. In the kitchen he laid her down on the carpet, and called. The house was empty. But a fire was burning.

Then again he kneeled to attend to her. She was breathing regularly, her eyes were wide open but there was something missing in her look. She was conscious in herself, but unconscious of her surroundings.

He ran upstairs, took blankets from a bed, and put them before the fire to warm. Then he removed her wet, mud-smelling clothing, rubbed her dry with a towel, and wrapped her in the blankets. Then he went into the dining room to look for some whisky. He drank a little himself, and put some into her mouth.

The effect was immediate. She looked straight into his face, as if she had been seeing him for some time, and yet had only just become conscious of him.

"Dr Fergusson?" she said.

"What?" he answered.

He was taking off his jacket, intending to find some dry

clothing upstairs. He couldn't bear the smell of the dead, muddy water, and he was afraid for his own health.

"What did I do?" she asked.

"Walked into the lake," he replied. He had begun to shake as if he were sick, and he could hardly attend to her. Her eyes remained directly on him, he seemed to be going dark in his mind, looking back at her helplessly. The trembling became quieter in him, his life came back to him, dark and unknowing, but strong again.

"Was I mad?" she asked, while her eyes fixed on him all the time.

"Maybe, for the moment," he replied. He felt quiet, because his strength had come back.

"Am I mad now?" she asked.

"Are you?" he thought a moment. "No," he answered truthfully, "I don't see that you are." He turned his face aside. He was afraid now, because he felt confused, and felt somehow that her power was stronger than his. And she continued to look at him all the time. "Can you tell me where I can find some dry things to put on?" he asked.

"Did you dive into the lake for me?" she asked.

"No," he answered. "I walked in, but I fell."

There was silence for a moment. He hesitated. He wanted to go upstairs and get into dry clothing. But there was another desire in him. And she seemed to hold him. His will seemed to have gone to sleep, and left him, standing there in front of her. But he felt warm inside himself. He didn't tremble at all, though his clothes were wet and cold.

"Why did you?" she asked.

"Because I didn't want you to do such a foolish thing," he said.

"It wasn't foolish," she said, still staring at him as she lay on the floor. "It was the right thing to do. *I* knew best, then."

"I'll go and change these wet things," he said. But still he couldn't move away from her, until she sent him. It was as if she held him in her hands, and he couldn't escape. Or perhaps he didn't want to.

Suddenly she sat up. She felt the blankets around her and

her eyes became wild as if looking for something. He stood still with fear. She saw her clothes lying spread around her.

"Who undressed me?" she asked, her eyes resting full on his face.

"I did," he replied, "to get you dry and comfortable."

For some moments she sat and stared at him terribly, her lips apart.

"Do you love me then?" she asked.

He could only stand and stare at her. His soul seemed to melt.

She moved forward on her knees, and put her arms round him, round his legs, as he stood there, pressing her breasts against his legs, holding him with a strange trembling certainty, pressing him to her face, her throat, as she looked up at him with flashing eyes, victorious in first possession.

"You love me," she said in a low voice. "You love me. I know you love me, I know."

And she was kissing his knees through the wet clothing, wildly kissing his knees, his legs.

He looked down at the wet hair, the wild, bare animal shoulders. He was astonished, confused and afraid. He had never thought of loving her. He had never wanted to love her. When he rescued her he was a doctor, and she was a patient. There was nothing personal in it. It was horrible to have her there kissing his legs. It disgusted him. And yet – and yet – he didn't have the power to break away.

She looked at him again with the same powerful look of love, and that same frightening light of victory in her eyes. Against the delicate flame which seemed to come from her face like a light, he was powerless. And yet he had never intended to love her. He had never intended. And something in him would not give in.

"You love me," she repeated. "You love me."

Her hands were pulling him, pulling him down to her. He was afraid, even a little horrified. For he had, really, no intention of loving her. Yet her hands were pulling him towards her. He put his hand out quickly to steady himself, and grasped her bare shoulder. A flame seemed to burn the hand that grasped the bare shoulder. He had no intention of loving her: he fought against yielding to her. It was horrible – and yet the touch of her shoulder was wonderful, the shining of her face was beautiful. Was she mad? He had a horror of yielding to her. Yet something in him ached also.

He had been staring at the door, away from her. But his hand remained on her shoulder. She had gone suddenly very still. He looked down at her. Her eyes were now wide with fear, with doubt, the light was dying from her face, a shadow of terrible greyness was returning. He couldn't bear the touch of the question in her eyes, and the look of death beyond the question.

With an inward groan he gave way and let his heart yield towards her. A sudden gentle smile came on his face. And her eyes, which never left his face, slowly, slowly, filled with tears. He watched the strange water rise in her eyes. And his heart seemed to burn and melt away in his breast.

He could not bear to look at her any more. He dropped on his knees and caught her head with his arms and pressed her face against his throat. She was very still. His heart, which seemed to have broken, was burning in his breast. And he felt her slow, hot tears wetting his throat. But he couldn't move.

He felt the hot tears wet his neck. Now, he could never let her head go away from his arms. He wanted to remain like that forever, with his heart hurting him in a pain that was also life to him. Without knowing, he was looking down on her damp, soft brown hair.

Then, suddenly, he smelt the horrible smell of that water. And at the same moment she pulled away and looked at him. Her eyes were deep and sad. He was afraid of them, and he grasped her to him, kissing her, not knowing what he was doing. He never wanted to have her eyes look like that again.

When she turned her face to him again, there was a terrible shining joy in her eyes, which really terrified him, and yet which he now wanted to see, because he feared the other look.

"You love me?" she said, rather uneasily.

"Yes." The word cost him a painful effort. Not because it wasn't true. But because it was too newly true, and saying it seemed to tear open again his newly-torn heart. And he hardly wanted it to be true even now.

She lifted her face to him, and he bent forward and kissed her on the mouth, gently, with the one kiss that said he crossed over to her. After the kiss, her eyes again slowly filled with tears. There was complete silence. The strange pain of his heart filled him again. That he should love her? That this was love! Him, a doctor! How they would laugh if they knew! It was terrible for him to think they might know.

In the pain of that thought he looked again at her. He saw a tear fall and his heart flamed hot. He saw for the first time that one of her shoulders was bare, he could just see one of her small breasts in the darkened room.

"Why are you crying?" he asked, in a changed voice.

She looked at him, and behind the tears the consciousness of her situation for the first time brought a dark look of shame to her eyes.

"I'm not crying, really," she said, watching him half frightened.

He reached his hand, and softly closed it on her bare arm.

"I love you! I love you!" he said in a soft, low voice, unlike himself.

She dropped her head. The touch of his hand on her arm unsettled her. She looked up at him.

"I want to go," she said. "I want to go and get you some dry things."

"Why?" he said. "I'm all right."

"But I want to go," she said. "And I want you to change your things."

He let her arm go, and she wrapped herself in the blanket, looking at him rather frightened. And still she did not rise.

"Kiss me," she said softly, sadly.

He kissed her quickly, half in anger.

Then, after a second, she rose nervously, all mixed up in the blanket. He watched her as she tried to wrap herself up so that she could walk. And as she went, he saw her feet and her white leg, and he tried to remember her as she was when he had wrapped her in the blanket. But then he didn't want to remember, because she had been nothing to him then.

A noise came from within the dark house. Then he heard her voice: "There are the clothes." He rose and went to the stairs to pick up the bundle she had thrown down. He came back to the fire to rub himself down and dress. He smiled at his own appearance when he had finished.

The fire was dying so he put on coal. The house was quite dark now except for the light of a street-lamp which shone in faintly from outside. He lit the gas lamps and gathered his wet things into a bundle in the corner.

It was six o'clock. He ought to go back to his duties. He waited and still she didn't come down. So he went to the stairs and called:

"I'll have to go."

Almost immediately he heard her coming down. She had on her best black cotton dress, and her hair was tidy, but still damp. She looked at him – and, in spite of herself, smiled.

"I don't like you in those clothes," she said.

"Do I look terrible?" he answered.

They were shy with each other.

"I'll make you some tea," she said.

"No, I must go."

"Do you have to?" And she looked at him again with wide, doubtful eyes. And again, from the pain of his breast, he knew how he loved her. He went and bent to kiss her, gently, with his heart's painful kiss.

"And my hair smells so horrible," she said with her voice trembling. "And I'm horrible, so horrible." And she broke into bitter, heartbroken crying. "You can't want to love me."

"Don't be silly, don't be silly," he said, trying to comfort her, kissing her, holding her in his arms. "I want you. I want to marry you, we're going to be married, quickly, quickly – tomorrow if I can."

But she only cried bitterly.

"I feel horrible. I feel I'm horrible to you."

"No, I want you, I want you," was all he answered, blindly, with that terrible voice which frightened her almost more than the horror she would feel if he did *not* want her.

The Blind Man

The effect of war is an important matter in this story.
As in Lady Chatterly's Lover, *Lawrence creates a character who*
has been badly wounded. The complicated relationship between
the three characters is, however, the most important thing.
Maurice tries to get very close to Bertie in a scene that makes
the reader ask, who is the more wounded? Maurice is blinded but
Bertie seems to be limited in a more important way. Between
these two men, the woman is torn. The story was written
in 1918, at the end of the First World War.

I SABEL PERVIN WAS LISTENING FOR TWO SOUNDS — for the sound of wheels on the drive outside and for the noise of her husband's footsteps in the hall. It was the late afternoon of a rainy November day. The trap had gone to fetch her dearest and oldest friend from the station. Her husband, who had been blinded in the war in France and who had a scar on his forehead, would soon be coming in.

Maurice had been home for a year now. He was totally blind. Yet they had been very happy. Grange Farm was Maurice's own place. The farm workers lived at the back of the house. Isabel lived with her husband in the comfortable rooms in front. She and he had been almost entirely alone together since he was wounded. They talked and sang and read together. She wrote about books for a newspaper and he worked a good deal on the farm – simple work, it is true, but it gave him satisfaction. He milked the cows, separated the cream, and attended to the pigs and horses. Life was still very full for the blind man, peaceful in darkness. With his wife he had a whole world, rich and real.

They were newly happy. He did not even regret the loss of his sight in these times of dark joy.

But sometimes the rich happiness would leave them. In that silent house, sometimes a sense of terrible weariness overcame Isabel. Then she felt she would go mad, for she could not bear it. And sometimes he was overcome with despair – a black misery, when his own life was unbearable to him. She tried to wrap herself up still further in her husband. She forced the old cheerfulness and joy to continue. But the effort that it cost her was almost too much. She felt she would scream, and would give anything, anything, to escape. When again he was sunk in blackest misery, she could not bear him, she could not bear herself.

She looked for a way out. She invited friends. She tried to give him some further connection with the outer world. But it was no good. Other people seemed shallow after their dark, great year of blindness and nearness.

But now, in a few weeks' time, her second baby would be born. The first had died when her husband went out to France. She looked with joy and relief to the coming of the second. But also she felt some anxiety. She was thirty years old. Her husband was a year younger. They both wanted the child very much. Yet she could not help feeling afraid. The child would occupy her love and attention. And then, what of Maurice? What would he do? She sighed with fear.

It was at this time that Bertie Reid wrote to Isabel. He was her old friend, a favourite cousin. All her life he had been her friend, like a brother, but better than her own brothers. She loved him – though not in the marrying sense.

Bertie was a lawyer, an intellectual type with a quick mind. Maurice was different. He was slow and sensitive – a big, heavy fellow. He was just the opposite to Bertie, whose mind was quicker than his feelings.

The two men had never liked each other. Isabel thought they *ought* to get on together. But they did not.

Therefore, when Maurice was going out to France, she wrote to Bertie saying that she must end her friendship with him.

For nearly two years nothing had passed between the two friends. Then a little note came from Bertie. He wrote of the real pain he felt about Maurice's loss of sight. Isabel felt nervous excitement again. And she read the letter to Maurice.

"Ask him to come down," he said.

"Ask Bertie to come here!"

"Yes – if he wants to."

Isabel paused for a few moments.

"I know he wants to," she replied. "But what about you, Maurice? How would you like it?"

"I should like it."

"Well – in that case – But I thought you didn't care for him – "

"Oh, I don't know. I might think differently of him now," the blind man replied.

So Bertie was coming, coming this evening, in the November rain and darkness. Isabel was restless. Her old feelings of anxiety and uncertainty returned. She looked nervously again at the high windows where the rain was beating against the glass. Why did these men not come? Ah, why had she no peace?

She rose to her feet and glanced at herself in the mirror. Her face was calm. Her neck made a beautiful line to her shoulder. She had a warm, motherly look.

She passed down the wide hall, put on heavy shoes, wrapped a large coat around her, put on a man's hat, and went out into the first yard. It was very dark. The wind was roaring in the great trees. When she came to the second yard, the darkness seemed deeper. She wished she had brought a lamp. Rain blew against her. She half liked it and she half felt that she did not want to struggle against it.

She reached the door to the stable. There was no light anywhere. She opened the door and looked in, into total darkness. The smell of horses and of warmth shocked her. She listened but could only hear the night and the small movement of a horse.

"Maurice!" she called softly. "Maurice – are you there?"

Nothing came from the darkness. She knew that the rain and the wind were blowing in upon the horses, the hot animal life. She entered and shut the door. She was conscious of the horses though she could not see them, and she was afraid.

Then she heard a small noise in the distance. It was Maurice in the other part of the stable. The low sound of his voice as he spoke to the horses came to her in the darkness.

She called quietly, "Maurice, Maurice – dear!"

"Yes," he answered. "Isabel?"

She saw nothing, and the sound of his voice seemed to touch her.

"Won't you come in, dear?" she said.

"Yes, I'm coming. Just half a minute. Bertie's not come yet, has he?"

"Not yet," said Isabel.

She wished he would come away. When she could not see him, she was afraid of him.

"Bertie won't much enjoy the drive in this weather," he said, as he closed the door.

"He won't indeed!" said Isabel calmly, watching the dark shape at the door.

"Give me your arm, dear," she said.

She pressed his arm to her as they went. She could feel the clever, careful, strong contact of his feet with the earth. For a moment he was a tower of darkness to her.

Isabel was glad when they entered the house. She was a little afraid of him out there. In the passage he sat down heavily. He was a man with powerful legs that seemed to know the earth. As he bent down to unfasten his boots, he didn't seem blind. When he stood up, the blood rushed to his face and neck, and she didn't look at his blindness.

He went away upstairs. She saw him go into the darkness. He did not know that the lamps upstairs were unlighted. He went on into the darkness with unchanging step. She heard him in the bathroom.

Maurice moved about almost unconsciously in his familiar surroundings. He seemed to know where objects were before he touched them. He didn't think much or trouble much. So long as he had the power of touch, he was happy without sight. It was a pleasure to stretch out his hand and meet an unseen object, to grasp it and possess it. He didn't try to remember what it had looked like. He didn't want to. The new way of consciousness had become natural to him. He was generally happy and he had a burning love for Isabel. But at times the flow of his life was broken. Then it would become a roaring sea, and he suffered in the disorder of his blood.

Tonight, however, he was still calm, though his nerves were a little sharp. He had to handle the razor carefully while he shaved. His hearing was also too sharp. He was conscious of all the sounds of the house. As he went to his room he heard the trap arrive.

Then came Isabel's voice like a bell ringing. "Is it you, Bertie?"

And a man's voice answered out of the wind. "Hello, Isabel. There you are. You're looking as fit as ever."

"Oh yes," said Isabel. "I'm wonderfully well. How are you? Rather thin, I think – ."

"Worked to death. But I'm all right. How's Maurice? Isn't he here?"

"Oh yes, he's upstairs, changing his clothes. Yes, he's well."

They moved away. Maurice heard no more. But a childish sense of despair had come over him. He seemed shut out – like a child that is left out. He dressed himself and went downstairs.

Isabel was alone in the dining room. She watched him enter.

"Did you hear Bertie come, Maurice?" she said.

"Yes – isn't he here?"

"He's in his room. He looks very thin and worn."

Bertie came down. He was a little dark man, with a very big forehead, thin hair, and sad, large eyes. He had odd, short legs. Isabel watched him hesitate at the door, and glance nervously at her husband.

Bertie went across to Maurice.

The blind man stuck his hand out and Bertie took it. Isabel glanced at them, and glanced away, as if she couldn't bear to see them.

"Come," she said. "Come to the table. Aren't you both hungry?"

They sat down.

Maurice felt for his place, his knife and fork. Bertie picked up a little bowl of violets from the table, and held them to his nose.

"They have a sweet scent," he said. "Where do they come from?"

"From the garden – under the windows. Bertie, do you remember the violets under Aunt Bell's wall?"

The two friends looked at each other and smiled.

The meal continued and Isabel and Bertie spoke easily together. The blind man was silent. He touched his food with quick, delicate touches of his knife. He could not bear to be helped.

After the meal, the three sat around the fire. Isabel put more logs on the fire and Bertie noticed a slight weariness in her movements.

"Will you be glad when the child comes, Isabel?" he said.

She looked at him with a smile.

"Yes, I shall be very glad. So will you, Maurice, won't you?" she added.

"Yes, I shall," replied her husband.

"We are both looking forward to it so much," she said.

"Yes, of course," said Bertie.

He was three or four years older than Isabel and had never married. He lived in beautiful rooms overlooking a river, and he had friends of the fair sex – but they were friends, not lovers. If they seemed to come too close, he pulled away. Isabel knew him very well, his beautiful kindness, but also his weakness which made him unable ever to enter into any close human contact. He was ashamed of himself because he couldn't marry. He wanted to do so. But he couldn't. At the centre of him he was afraid. He had given up hope and no longer expected to escape his own weakness.

He became a successful lawyer, a rich man and a great social success. But at the centre he felt himself nothing.

Isabel looked at his sad face and his little short legs. She looked at his dark grey eyes. There was something child-like in him and she loved him. At the same time his weakness was pitiable and disgusting to her. He understood this.

Suddenly, Bertie spoke to Maurice.

"Isabel tells me that you have not suffered unbearably from the loss of sight."

Maurice straightened himself but kept his arms folded.

"No," he said, "not unbearably. You stop worrying about many things."

Maurice stretched the strong muscles of his back and leaned backwards.

"And that is a relief," said Bertie. "But what is there in the place of the worry? What replaces the activity? When there is no thought and no action, there is nothing."

Maurice was slow in replying.

"There is something," Maurice replied. "I couldn't tell you what it is."

Then the blind man was silent. He rose restlessly, a big, awkward, uncomfortable figure. He wanted to go away.

"Do you mind," he said, "if I go and speak to the farm manager?"

"No – go along, dear," said Isabel.

And he went out. A silence came over the two friends. The wind blew loudly outside. Rain beat like a drum on the windows. The logs burned slowly with hot small flames. Bertie seemed uneasy. There were dark circles around his eyes. Isabel leaned and looked into the fire.

"The child coming seems to make me calm. I can't feel there's anything to trouble about," she said.

"A good thing, I should say," Bertie replied slowly.

"I wish I felt that I needn't trouble about Maurice. Then I'd be quite content."

The evening passed slowly. Isabel looked at the clock.

"I say," she said. "It's nearly ten o'clock. Where can Maurice be?"

Bertie looked at her. "Would you like me to go out and see?"

"Well – if you wouldn't mind. I'd go, but –" She did not want to make the effort.

Bertie put on an old overcoat and took a lamp. He went out from the side door. He felt nervous and strangely empty. Unwillingly, he went through the wet and roaring night. A dog barked violently at him.

At last, he opened the door of a stable and, looking in, he saw Maurice standing, listening.

"Who is that?" said Maurice.

"It's me," said Bertie.

A large, half-wild grey cat was rubbing at Maurice's leg. The blind man bent to rub its sides. Bertie watched the scene, then entered and shut the door behind him.

Maurice straightened himself.

"You came to look for me?" he said.

"Isabel was a little worried," said Bertie.

"I'll come in."

"I hope I'm not in your way at all," said Bertie, rather shy and stiff.

"My way?" Maurice said. "Not a bit. I'm glad Isabel has somebody to talk to. I'm afraid that *I* am in the way. I know I'm not very lively company. Is Isabel all right, do you think? She's not unhappy, is she?"

"I don't think so."

"What does she say?"

"She says she's very content – only a little troubled about you. She's afraid you might become miserable," Bertie said cautiously.

"She needn't worry about that. I'm afraid that she'll find me a dead weight, always alone with me down here."

Maurice dropped his voice curiously. "I say," he asked, secretly struggling, "is my face a very ugly sight? Do you mind telling me?"

"There is the scar," Bertie said, wondering. "But it is more pitiable than shocking."

"A bad scar, though," said Maurice.

70

"Oh, yes."

There was a pause.

"Sometimes I feel that I am horrible," said Maurice, in a low voice. And Bertie actually felt a wave of horror.

"That's nonsense," he said.

"I don't really know you, do I?" Maurice said in a strange voice.

"Probably not," said Bertie.

"Do you mind if I touch you?"

Bertie pulled away instinctively but he said, in a small voice, "Not at all."

He suffered as the blind man stretched out a strong naked hand. He laid it on Bertie's head in a soft, firm grasp, gathering it. Then he moved his hand and softly closed it again until he had covered the face of the smaller man, touching the forehead, the closed eyes, the small nose, the rough, short moustache, the mouth, the strong jaw.

"You seem young," Maurice said quietly, at last.

Bertie stood nearly destroyed, unable to answer.

"Your head seems tender, as if you were young," Maurice repeated. "So do your hands. Touch my eyes, will you? Touch my scar."

Bertie shook with disgust. Yet he was under the power of the blind man. He lifted his hand, and laid the fingers on the scar. Maurice suddenly covered them with his own hand, pressed the fingers of the other man upon his scarred eyes, his body trembling. He remained thus for a minute or more while Bertie stood as if unconscious, imprisoned.

Then, suddenly Maurice removed the hand of the other man and stood holding it in his own.

"Oh my God," he said. "We shall know each other now, shan't we? We shall know each other now."

Bertie could not answer. He stared silently and in terror, overcome by his own weakness. He knew that he could not answer. He had an unreasonable fear that the other man would suddenly destroy him. Maurice was actually filled with a burning desire for friendship – and Bertie fled from it.

"It's all right now, as long as we live. We're all right together now, aren't we?" Maurice said.

"Yes," said Bertie trying to escape.

Maurice stood with his head lifted. Then he turned for his coat.

"Come," he said, "we'll go to Isabel."

Bertie took the lamp and opened the door. The two men went in silence.

Isabel heard their footsteps and looked up anxiously as they entered. There seemed a curious happiness in Maurice. Bertie looked tired. His eyes were dark and sunken.

"What is it?" she asked

"We've become friends," said Maurice.

She looked at Bertie. He met her eyes with a despairing look. His eyes were full of misery.

"I'm so glad," she said in complete confusion.

"Yes," said Maurice.

Isabel took his hand with both of hers and held it tight.

"You'll be happier now, dear," she said.

But she was watching Bertie. She knew that he had one desire — to escape from this friendship which had been forced upon him. He could not bear the thought that he had been touched by the blind man. He was like a shellfish whose shell is broken.

Mother and Daughter

*The story was written in 1928 just two years before
Lawrence's death. In some ways, it is rather a cruel story in that
each character, in a different way, will probably suffer. However,
no single character is very likeable. The relationship between
mother and daughter is the most important in the story. Like
most relationships in Lawrence, it is based upon power. Lawrence
also shows how the younger woman is pulled out of the power of
the female and towards that of the male. But the real mastery of
Lawrence in this story is shown by the way he moves the reader
between the thoughts and feelings of the various characters
without making any one of them particularly attractive.*

VIRGINIA BODOIN HAD A GOOD JOB; she was head of a
department in a government office and earned seven
hundred and fifty pounds a year. Rachel Bodoin, her
mother, received about six hundred pounds a year from
the money that her husband had left her. Since the death
of that never very important person, she had lived comfort-
ably in the capitals of Europe.

Now, after some years of separation and "freedom",
mother and daughter once more thought of settling down.
They had become, in time, more like a married couple than
mother and daughter. They knew one another very well
indeed, and each was a little "nervous" of the other. They
had lived together and parted several times. Virginia was
now thirty, and she didn't look like marrying. For four years
she had lived with Henry Lubbock, a rather spoilt young
man who was musical. Then Henry let her down for two
reasons. He couldn't stand her mother, and her mother
couldn't stand him. And when Mrs Bodoin didn't like
someone, she made it very clear. And Virginia, in a helpless

sort of family loyalty, began to treat Henry badly. She didn't really want to but she couldn't help it. For her mother had power over her; a strange *female* power that had nothing to do with her being a parent. So that was one of Henry's reasons for leaving Virginia.

The second reason was that Virginia had no money except what she earned. Henry earned almost nothing from his music and he knew that he would find it hard to earn more. So marrying, except with a wife who could keep him, was rather out of the question. Virginia would one day get her mother's money, but Mrs Bodoin was very strong and healthy. She would live forever, making his life miserable. Henry lived with Virginia for four years as if they were married, and Virginia *felt* they were married, except for a small ceremony. But she had her mother always in the background; often as far back as Paris or Biarritz, but still, within reach by letter.

In the end, Henry left. He was fond of Virginia and he could hardly manage without her, and he was sorry for her. But at length he couldn't see her apart from her mother. She was young and weak and held in her mother's grasp.

Henry met other women, got into another relationship, and gradually worked his way away from Virginia. He saved his life, but he had lost, he felt, a good deal of his youth and courage.

Virginia blamed her mother and Mrs Bodoin blamed Virginia for letting Henry escape and for becoming too friendly with him in the first place. For five years they kept apart from each other. But the spell was not broken. Mrs Bodoin's mind never left her daughter, and Virginia was always conscious of her mother, somewhere in the world. They wrote, and met at times, but they kept part of themselves apart.

The spell, however, was between them, and gradually it worked. They felt more friendly. Mrs Bodoin came to London. She stayed in the same quiet hotel with her daughter: Virginia had had two rooms in an hotel for the past three years. And, at last, they thought of taking a flat together.

Virginia was now over thirty. She was still thin and a little strange, almost like a child. She still had her twisted smile and her slow, rather deep voice, that made a man feel that he was being softly touched by her fingertips. Her hair was still natural, full of untidy curls. She still dressed in good expensive clothes though there was something untidy about her. She still might have a hole in her expensive and perfectly new stockings, and she still might have to take her shoes off when she came to tea because they were too tight. If she bought a good pair of simple and natural shoes, made to her size, the shoes would start to hurt her when she had walked half a mile in them. She nearly always wore her mother's old shoes. "Of course, I go through life in mother's old shoes. If she died and left me without a supply, I suppose I'd have to go in a wheelchair," she would say, with her strange twisted little smile. She was so smart and yet untidy. It was her charm, really.

Mrs Bodoin was very different. She was one of those women of sixty or so, with a terrible inner energy. But she managed to hide it. She sat with a perfect calm, and folded hands. But she was really like a volcano at rest that might explode at any minute.

She didn't try to hide her grey hair or her age. She studied her face and decided to accept her appearance. She was an independent woman and she decided not to be either young or attractive. She would keep her pride, for she was fond of it. She was determined. She liked to be determined. She was used to being determined. She would just *be* determined.

She looked like someone from the eighteenth century with her silver-white hair brushed straight back from her forehead. She had a rather full, pink face and strong, independent eyes. Her whole body showed that she was energetic but very calm, and very determined.

She had two thousand pounds that she could spare. Virginia was always in debt. But, after all, Virginia earned seven hundred and fifty pounds a year which was an attractive amount of money.

Virginia was strangely clever and not clever. She didn't _really_ know anything deeply, because anything and everything was interesting to her for the moment, and she picked it up at once. She learnt languages very easily and could speak them in two weeks. This helped her greatly in her job. But she didn't really _know_ any language, not even her own. She picked things up in her sleep, so to speak, without knowing anything about them.

And this made her very popular with men. She worked with men, spent most of her time with men, her friends were nearly all men. She didn't feel easy with women. Yet she had no lover, nobody seemed eager to marry her, nobody seemed eager to come close to her at all. Mrs Bodoin said: "I'm afraid Virginia is a one-man woman. I am a one-man woman. Virginia's father was the only man in my life, the only one. And I'm afraid Virginia is the same."

Henry had said in the past that Mrs Bodoin wasn't a one-man woman, she was a no-man woman, and that if she could have her way, everything male would be wiped off the face of the earth, and only females would be left.

However, Mrs Bodoin thought that it was now time to act. So she and Virginia took a beautiful flat in one of the better areas of London. They furnished it well and set up married life together, mother and daughter.

At first, it was very exciting. Virginia, for the first time in her life, had the pleasure of making a home. She was again entirely under her mother's spell. She had had no idea that her mother had such treasures as the carpets, the grey and gold chairs, the rich, beautiful furniture. Almost like a child, like a girl newly-married, Virginia threw herself into the business of arranging the rooms. "Of course, Virginia, I consider that this is _your_ flat," said Mrs Bodoin. "I shall carry out your wishes entirely."

Of course Virginia had a few wishes, but not many. She bought some wild pictures from poor artists she knew. Mrs Bodoin didn't like them but she let them stay. She looked on them as part of the ugliness of the modern world.

The mother and daughter, the mother in a sort of dark,

faded red and the daughter in silver, began to entertain. They had, of course, mostly men. So there were dinners and well-arranged evenings.

It went well, but something was missing. Mrs Bodoin wanted to be gracious, so she held herself rather back. She was a little distant, calm, wanting Virginia to be the centre of attention. But it didn't work. It stopped something. She was very nice with the men, no matter what she really felt about them. But the men were uneasy with her, afraid.

What they all felt, all the men guests, was that *for them*, nothing really happened. Everything that happened was between mother and daughter. All the flow was between mother and daughter. A spell joined the two women and, however hard they tried, the men were shut out. More than one young man *began* to fall in love with Virginia. But it was impossible. Not only was he shut out, he was, in some way, destroyed.

It was terrible. Because Mrs Bodoin wanted Virginia to fall in love and marry. She really wanted it and she blamed Virginia's attitude on Henry. She never understood that the spell was on her as well as Virginia, and that it made men just an impossibility to both women, mother and daughter alike.

At this time she tried to hide her rather cruel sense of humour. It destroyed the objects of her humour, broke them as if they had been hit with a hammer. It frightened people, particularly men. It frightened men off.

So she hid it. She hid it. But it was there, this hammer-like humour which just hit its object on the head and left him destroyed. She tried to pretend, even to Virginia, that this weapon was gone; but the hammer was there, hidden, and every guest felt fear, and Virginia felt a little smile on her face as still another fool male was knocked on the head. It was a sort of strange sport.

No, the plan was not going to work: the plan of having Virginia fall in love and marry. But there was one man, at least, that Mrs Bodoin had real hopes of. He was a healthy and very good-looking boy of good family, with no money, and not very clever, but simply in love with Virginia's cleverness. True, he was twenty-six, to Virginia's thirty-one. But he simply loved her cleverness. To Adrian, Virginia had the finest mind on earth. He loved her on his knees, but because she was a woman he felt that he could protect her.

"Of course, he's just a very nice *boy*!" said Mrs Bodoin. "He's a boy, and that's all you can say. And he always will be a boy. But that's the very nicest kind of man, the only kind you can live with. Virginia, aren't you attracted to him?"

"Yes, mother! I think he's a terribly nice *boy*, as you say," replied Virginia, in her rather low, musical voice. But the mocking curl of her voice meant the end of Adrian. Virginia was not marrying a nice *boy*! She could fight too, against her mother's taste. And Mrs Bodoin became impatient.

She had made her own plans, planning to give Virginia the flat and half of her money if she married Adrian. Yes, the mother was already working out her future life, when Virginia was happily married to that most attractive if rather brainless *boy*.

A year later, when Virginia was thirty-two, Adrian, who had married a rich American girl, came to see Virginia. He knelt faithfully at her feet and felt faithfully that she was the most wonderful, spiritual person, who could have done wonders for him, except that it was too late for he was already married.

Virginia was looking worn and tired. She was as thin as a rail. Her nerves were very bad and she could never forget her job. She used to come home at tea-time speechless and worn out. Mrs Bodoin could not stop worrying about Virginia even though that made Virginia's nerves worse.

Mrs Bodoin had always disliked Virginia's job. But now she hated it. She violently hated the whole government office. It was turning her daughter into a thin, complaining woman. When she heard Virginia's key in the lock, she would quickly hurry into one of the other rooms until her daughter had safely passed. It was too much for poor Virginia's nerves even to catch sight of anybody in the house when she came in from the office.

And Mrs Bodoin would wonder: How is she? How is she tonight? I wonder what sort of day she's had? And this thought would wander through the house, to where Virginia was lying on her back in her room. At dinner she would appear with black lines under her eyes, thin and bad-tempered, a young woman out of an office, unable to eat, uninterested in anything.

Mrs Bodoin was longing for an evening with some life in it. But Virginia would simply sit listening to the same record over and over again.

During the second terrible year, Mrs Bodoin knew she was beaten. She was a woman without object or meaning any more. The hammer of her female humour, which had knocked so many people on the head, had at last flown backwards and hit her. For her daughter was her other self. The secret and the meaning and the power of Mrs Bodoin's whole life lay in the hammer, that hammer of her living humour which knocked everything on the head. And she had hoped to hand on the hammer to Virginia, her clever daughter, her other self. But Virginia had had a father and one fact gradually became clear to Mrs Bodoin: Virginia was her father's daughter. Robert Bodoin had been fully and deservedly knocked on the head by her hammer and, now, it was disgusting that he should live again in the person of her own daughter.

The two women were now mostly alone. Virginia was too tired to have company in the evening. So there was the record player or else the silence. Both women had come to hate the flat. Virginia longed again for her two small rooms in the hotel. She hated the flat: she hated everything. But she hadn't the energy to move. She hadn't the energy to do anything. She struggled to work, and when she got home, she lay down, tired out.

It was Virginia's worn-out state and lack of energy that really finished Mrs Bodoin. She had tried to persuade Virginia to give up her work. She had offered her half of her money. In vain. Virginia stuck to her office.

Very well! So be it!

"Virginia, don't you think we'd better get rid of this flat, and live as we used to? Don't you think we should do that?" she said, when she couldn't bear it any more.

"But what about all the money you've put into it?" cried Virginia.

"Never mind!" said Mrs Bodoin. "We had the pleasure of making it. And we've had as much pleasure out of living in it as we shall ever have. Now we'd better get rid of it – quickly – don't you think?"

Mrs Bodoin's arms were trembling with the desire to pack and go.

"Let's wait till Sunday before we decide," said Virginia.

"Till Sunday! Four days! As long as that? Haven't we already decided in our own minds?" said Mrs Bodoin.

"We'll wait till Sunday, anyhow," said Virginia.

The next evening, the Turk came to dinner. Virginia called him Arnold. Mrs Bodoin, who disliked him immediately, could never remember his second name. She called him simply the Turkish Delight after the soft sweet.

Virginia had seen a good deal of the Turk at the office where she worked with him on a government trade agreement. So the friendship had followed the formal business.

He was sixty, grey-haired and fat. He had many grandchildren in his own country, but he was a widower. He had a grey moustache cut like a brush, and dark brown eyes over which heavy lids hung. His manner was humble, but he had a certain determined pride. He had been very wealthy and then he had been ruined, but now he was rising again, his sons at home backing him. One felt he was not alone. He had his sons, his family, his tribe behind him, away in Turkey.

He spoke bad English but fairly good French. He didn't speak much, but he sat. He sat, with his short, fat legs, as if for ever, *there*. There was a strange power in his fat motionlessness, as if he were connected with the very centre of the earth. And his brain, spinning away at the one point in question, business, was very lively. Business kept him fully busy. But not in a nervous, personal way. Somehow the family, the tribe was always felt behind him. It was business for the family, the tribe.

With the English he was humble, for the English like such people to be humble. And he was always an outsider. Nobody would ever take any notice of him in society. He would just be an outsider, *sitting*.

"I hope, Virginia, you won't ask that man when we have other company. I can bear it," said Mrs Bodoin, "but other people might mind."

"It's hard when you can't choose your own company in your own house," mocked Virginia.

"I don't care," said Mrs Bodoin. "But I don't suppose you look upon him as a personal friend – ?"

"I do. I like him quite a lot."

Mrs Bodoin was horrified this time. She looked on the Turk as being outside the class of human beings, and in the class of insects. That he had been very rich, and might be again, only added to her feeling of disgust at having to have him in her flat.

However, she was not quite just. True, he was fat, and he sat, with short legs in animal silence. His colour was of a dirty sort of paste, his eyes heavy. And he never spoke until spoken to, waiting in his animal's silence, like a slave.

But his thick, white hair, which stood up on his head like a soft brush, was strangely alive. And his small hands, of the same soft dull paste, had a peculiar, fat, soft, male life of their own. And his dull brown eyes could shine with intelligence under the heavy white lids. He was tired but he was not defeated. He had fought, and won, and lost, and was fighting again.

At dinner he sat humbly but with the pride of the humble. His manners were perfectly good, rather French. Virginia spoke easily to him in that language while Mrs Bodoin struggled to understand. It wasn't his fault that French was being spoken. It was Virginia's.

He was very humble with Mrs Bodoin. But he sometimes looked at her as if to say: "Yes! I see you. You are a fine figure. But what are you as a woman? You are neither wife nor mother nor lover. You have no scent of sex. No man would touch you." And he would secretly pray to his gods to protect himself from her.

Yet he was in love with Virginia. He saw first the child in her, as if she were a lost child waiting for someone to pick her up. A fatherless child! And he was a tribal father, a father through all the ages.

Then, on the other hand, he knew her peculiar cleverness in business. He was deeply attracted by it. It seemed to him very strange. But it would be an immense help to him. He did not really understand the English. But she could help him. For she was, after all, an important person among these English, these English officials.

He was about sixty. His family was in Turkey. It was necessary for him to live in England for some years. The girl would be useful. She had no money except what she would get from her mother. But she would help his business. And then the flat. He liked the flat very much. And then she was almost innocent. The English knew nothing of his sort of Eastern male sexuality. And, last of all, he was lonely, getting old and tired.

Virginia of course didn't know why she liked being with Arnold. She was stupid in matters of real life, of living. She said he was "amusing". She found his business "interesting", and his dark shining eyes under the white, thick lids made her feel helpless as a woman. She saw him quite often, had tea with him in his hotel, and drove with him one day down to the sea.

When he took her hand in his soft still hands, she trembled with fear, she was helpless. He was so strange and strong, he seemed to have all the power. He didn't just want to make love to her: he wanted to marry her. And he must make himself master of her. And he drew nearer to her.

She leaned against his breast and let him touch her. She thought for a second of her mother. Then she felt in the air the sense of fate, fate. Oh, so nice, not to have to struggle. To give way to fate. She agreed to marry him and said that he must tell her mother. And while she hid her face against his breast, his male pride felt its victory.

Mrs Bodoin had no idea that Virginia had been alone with the Turkish Delight. She did not inquire into her daughter's movements. During the famous dinner, she was calm and withdrawn. When, after coffee, Virginia left her alone with the Turkish Delight, she made no effort at conversation. She only glanced with dislike at the short, fat man.

"Mrs Bodoin," he said at last, "I want to ask you something."

"You do? Then why not ask it?" she said in a cold, uninterested voice.

"Yes! It is this. I would like to marry your daughter. She is willing to take me."

There was a moment's pause.

"What was that, that you said?" she asked. "Repeat it!"

"I would like to marry your daughter. She is willing to take me."

His dark eyes looked at her, then glanced away again. Leaning forward, she stared fixedly at him, as if under a spell, turned to stone.

"I think we'll wait till she comes," Mrs Bodoin said, leaning back.

There was silence. She stared at the ceiling. He looked closely round the room, at the furniture, the curtains.

"I will give Miss Virginia five thousand pounds on our marriage," came his voice. "She will, I think, have this flat."

Absolute silence. He might as well have been on the moon. But he was a good sitter. He just sat until Virginia came in.

Mrs Bodoin was still staring at the ceiling. The iron had at last fully entered her soul. Virginia glanced at her, but said:

"Have a drink, Arnold?"

He rose and came towards the sideboard, and stood beside her while she poured his drink. Then they came to their chairs.

"Arnold has spoken to you, mother?" said Virginia.

Mrs Bodoin sat up straight, and stared at Virginia with big, anxious eyes. Virginia was terrified, yet a little excited. Her mother was beaten.

"Is it true, Virginia, that you are *willing* to marry this – this man?" asked Mrs Bodoin slowly.

"Yes, mother, quite true," said Virginia, in her mocking, soft voice.

Mrs Bodoin looked wide-eyed and confused.

"May I be excused from having anything to do with it – or with him?" she asked in a slow, clear voice.

"Why, of course!" said Virginia, frightened, smiling strangely.

There was a pause. Then Mrs Bodoin, feeling old and tired, pulled herself together again.

"And I understand that your future husband would like to have this flat?" came her voice.

"Well – perhaps!" said Virginia. "Perhaps he would like to know that I possessed it."

Arnold nodded gravely.

"And do you wish to possess it?" came Mrs Bodoin's slow voice. "Do you intend to *live* here, with your *husband*?"

"Yes, I think so," said Virginia. "You know you *said* the flat was mine, mother."

"Very well! As you wish. I'll send my lawyer to this – this Eastern gentleman, if you will leave written instructions on my table. May I ask when you are thinking of getting – *married*?"

"What do you think, Arnold?" said Virginia.

"Shall it be in two weeks?" he said, sitting straight, with his hands on his knees.

"In about two weeks, mother," said Virginia.

"I've heard. In two weeks! Very well! Everything will be settled by then. And now, please excuse me." She rose, made a slight general bow, and moved calmly from the room. It was killing her, that she could not scream aloud and beat the Turk out of the house. But she couldn't. She had forced herself into control.

Arnold stood and looked with shining eyes around the

room. It would be his. When his sons came to England, here he would receive them.

He looked at Virginia. She too was white and weary now. And she had turned away from him as if suffering for the defeat of her mother. He knew she might still change her mind.

"Your mother is a wonderful lady," he said, going to Virginia and taking her hand. "But she has no husband to shelter her, she is unfortunate. I would be happy if she would like to stay here with us."

He knew exactly the right thing to say.

"I'm afraid there's no hope of that," said Virginia with that strange, mocking smile.

They sat together and he touched her gently, softly almost like a father. And the strangeness of it, there in her mother's room, amused her. And because he saw that the things in the room were beautiful and valuable, his blood flamed and he held the thin girl tightly, because she represented these valuable surroundings, and brought them into his possession. And he said: "And you will be very comfortable, very content with me, very content, oh, I shall make you content, not like your mother. And you will get fatter and grow like a rose. I shall make you grow like the rose. And shall we marry next week, next Wednesday? Wednesday is a good day. Shall it be then?"

"Very well!" said Virginia, giving in to her fate, having to make no more effort, no more effort, all her life.

Mrs Bodoin moved into an hotel next day, and came to the flat to pack only when Virginia was out. She and her daughter communicated only by letter, when it was necessary.

And in five days she was clear. All business that could be settled was settled, all her luggage was removed. She would go to Paris, to live out the rest of her days.

The last day she waited until Virginia came home. She sat there in her hat and street things, like a stranger.

"I just waited to say goodbye," she said. "I'm leaving in the morning for Paris. This is my address. I think everything is settled; if not, let me know and I'll attend to it. Well, goodbye! – and I hope you'll be *very happy*!"

She dragged out the last words almost like a threat.

"Why, I think I may be," said Virginia, with the twist of a smile.

"I wouldn't be surprised," said Mrs Bodoin pointedly and darkly. "I think the Turkish grandfather knows very well what he's doing. You're just his type of woman after all – someone out of his harem." The words came slowly, dropping, each with a plop! of deep disgust.

"I suppose I am! Rather fun!" said Virginia. "But I wonder where I got it from? Not from you, mother – " There was laughter in her voice.

"I should say *not*."

"Perhaps daughters are the opposites of their mothers," said Virginia wickedly. "All that type of woman – all the harem – was left out of you, so perhaps it all had to be put back into me."

Mrs Bodoin flashed a look at her.

"You have *all* my *pity*!" she said.

"Thank you, dear. You have just a bit of mine."

Glossary

brooch   an ornament on a woman's clothes, fastened with a pin

bruise   a discoloured place on the skin, caused by a blow

chrysanthemum   a garden plant with large brightly-coloured flowers

contact   touch; close relations

couple   a man and woman together, especially husband and wife

forehead   the part of the face above the eyes

harem   the women in a Muslim house

military   of a soldier; of an army

pond   a very small lake

scar   a mark on the skin, where a wound has healed

sleeve   the arm of a piece of clothing

spell   a condition caused by magical power

stable   a building in which horses are kept

stretcher   a flat covered framework for carrying a sick person

trap   a light two-wheeled vehicle, drawn by a horse

valentine   a greetings card sent (usually unsigned) to arrive on February 14th, St Valentine's Day, declaring one's love

volcano   a mountain with a deep hole in the top, from which smoke and red-hot rock may pour

Questions

The White Stocking

1 Why does Elsie get up earlier than usual at the beginning of the story?

2 What feelings does Elsie have as she watches Ted wash himself?

3 How does Ted feel about Elsie while he is at work?

4 How would you describe the feelings of Elsie and Sam as they dance together?

5 Why does Elsie cry after the dance?

6 "They both trembled in the balance." What do you think Lawrence means?

7 Who do you think is to blame for the attack on Elsie?

8 Who is the stronger, Elsie or Ted?

The Shadow in the Rose Garden

1 How does Lawrence first show that the wife is not really thinking about her husband?

2 What does Mrs Coates think about the relationship between the two of them?

3 Why is the garden described as "the magic beyond the doorway"?

4 Why does the woman want to visit the garden?

5 What is the gap between the husband and wife at the end?

6 Can you explain the title?

7 Do you think their marriage will last after this?

8 Was the woman 'right' to visit the garden, and was her husband right to feel jealous?

Odour of Chrysanthemums

1 Why does Lawrence write that the flames from the chimneys were "like red sores"?

2 What does the conversation between Elizabeth and her father tell us about her husband?

3 How do the children feel as they wait for their father's return?

4 How would you describe life in the mining village?

5 How does Elizabeth feel by the end of the story?

6 What are the differences between Elizabeth's reaction and the mother-in-law's?

7 What does Elizabeth feel when she looks at her husband's dead body?

8 Does Lawrence have a view of death in this story?

The Prussian Officer

1 Why do the officer's feelings towards the servant change?

2 What sort of relationship does the officer have with women?

3 Why does the officer kick the servant?

4 What makes the servant attack him?

5 What do the mountains represent to the dying servant?

6 Can you explain the officer's behaviour?

7 The servant is described as being like an "animal". In what ways do you think this is true?

8 Why are flame and fire mentioned so much in the story?

The Horse Dealer's Daughter

1 What makes Mabel different from her brothers?

2 Why is Joe compared to the horses?

3 Describe Mabel's feelings towards her father.

4 Why does Mabel decide to kill herself?

5 How do Dr Fergusson's feelings towards Mabel change?

6 Both Mabel and Dr Fergusson are described as being frightened at the end. Why do you think this is?

7 What different types of men are described in the story?

8 Do you agree with Lawrence's view of love in this story?

The Blind Man

1 Why does Isabel invite friends to the house?

2 Compare the characters of Maurice and Bertie.

3 How does Maurice manage with his blindness?

4 What do you think is missing from Bertie's life?

5 What does Bertie feel when Maurice touches him?

6 At the end of the story what do each of the characters think has happened?

7 "You'll be happier now, dear." Is Isabel right?

8 Which character in the story has your greatest sympathy?

Mother and Daughter

1 "They had become ... more like a married couple than mother and daughter." What does Lawrence mean by that?

2 Why does Henry leave Virginia?

3 How can Virginia be "strangely clever and not clever"?

4 Why is Mrs Bodoin's humour like a "hammer"?

5 Why doesn't Virginia like Adrian?

6 What attracts Virginia to Arnold?

7 Which character in the story is the most likeable?

8 Do you think the marriage will be a happy one?

General

1 Some women critics dislike the way Lawrence represents women. Do you agree with them?

2 What do these stories tell you about English society at that time?

3 Which do you think is the best story?

4 What do you think is the most important idea Lawrence gives us in this collection?

5 Who have greater power in these stories – the men or the women?